ONE HEART ONE MIND

MEMORIES FROM MY YEAR IN VIETNAM
JULY 1970–71

J.J. CARNEY

Gender Liberation Press LLC
PO Box 7709
Seminole Florida 33775

www.facebook.com/genderliberationpress

Edited by Kitty Werbey

With deep thanks
To my dear friend Ricki Liff
For supporting my writing

ISBN 978-0-9911688-0-4

Introduction

It has been more than 25 years since the day I left Vietnam. Most of that time I have been either high or under the influence of alcohol. For those twenty-two-and-a-half years I have done my best to bury memories of the war. On August 20, 1993, I put the bottle down and made up my mind to write.

It has not been easy to deal with the emotions that these memories bring up, but it is something I feel I have to do. Some of the occurrences I can recall like they happened yesterday, others are coming back slowly. To the best of my memory what follows is my tour of Vietnam from July 1970 to July 1971.

There is no structure on when things happened, no structure in any order of time or actual sequence of events during the year, just a restructure of my year in Vietnam as I recall events of the year. These are just bits and pieces of what seemed important to me, and how I remember them with a touch of poetic license.

As all old Veterans know, war stories are odd things the storyteller, over the years, tends to mix a little added drama to each tale, yet some are one-hundred percent as they happened. If I help one person understand what the impact of the Vietnam War was on a twenty-year-old kid, I will be happy knowing that I have accomplished something with my life.

—J.J. Carney
(Written in 1996)

Foreword

I have known John Carney for many years and am honored by his request that I write a foreword to his fine book.

The Vietnam War has produced many memoirs, but very few have been published which speak for the experience of the overwhelming majority of troops that were there — the troops who were in support units, rather than combat units. My impression is that if a Martian wondered what the composition of American forces in Vietnam was, and used published memoirs as a guide, this Martian would conclude a million Special Forces, a million Army Airborne troopers, a million Marine riflemen, and perhaps a dozen of everyone else.

War does terrible things to people. The grief of loss is as painful when the person dead is the mailman' s assistant and the bullet a Viet Cong sniper's bullet, as if the dead man is an infantryman and the bullet shot by an NVA regular. The burdens of guilt — which we who never served in a war zone helplessly declare to be irrational — assumed for enemy atrocities against defenseless people, no less crushing in the soul of a mailman than that of an elite trooper. No person's suffering is commensurable with any other person's. It is time we dropped all pissing contests over who suffered more — and over who came through what unscarred.

I have known John Carney as a person with an enjoyable sense of humor, but did not know, until reading this book, his capacity for comic surprise and his unassuming knack of making the unhistoric, unheroic, and unelite — unforgettable. It is a pleasure to introduce readers to it.

—Jonathan Shay, M.D., Ph.D. Author of *Achilles in Vietnam: Combat Trauma and the Undoing of Character*

Contents

"The Day I arrived in Vietnam"
(part one of a poem)

July 14, 1970 was the day I arrived in Vietnam, I was so scared

I was so young

a bus from The Presidio of San Francisco to the Oakland Airport

a quiet nervous flight to our first layover in Hawaii

a planeload of young boys hoarded into a lounge underage, yet we are allowed one drink

Military Police block every door

no last chance to desert, to say never mind,

or to disappear into the Hawaii Beaches.

The last layover Okinawa, no alcohol here

just heat, dust and soda machines, nowhere to run or hide

an hour later we are back on board,

then circling Ton Son Nhut Airport

a planeload of scared young men, more boys then men.

As we circle the Airport the Captain says:

"Welcome to Vietnam, enjoy your stay"

we do not appreciate the humor

the captain continues "Once we land…

head as fast you can into the terminal

we will unload and reload rather rapidly."

we race to the old terminal built by the French in the 1920's

we claim our duffel bags and are boarded onto buses

so young, so scared, all playing the tough guy

the bus has mesh metal screen over the windows

we learn quickly as to protect us from rocks tossed by the local children

we pass a pile of dead Vietcong, in black P J's

Welcome to Saigon, Welcome to Vietnam

we were so scared, we were so young.

We are once again quickly unloaded off the buses

in the morning, we will receive our duty assignments

based on our military occupational training

we are given a cot, a pillow, sheets, a hot meal of sorts

the assignment center is like an old western town

wooden sidewalks over the mud

wooden buildings with tin roofs, bags of sand keep the tin roofs on

I cling to the only person I know

we had hung out at the Presidio playing eight ball for drinks

he declares that from now on his name is Jesse James.

I laugh, and say well that makes me Billy the Kid

we are in search of some of that famous Vietnamese marijuana we have heard so much about

we do not find any

exhausted we go back to our cots and a restless night's sleep.

We were so scared, we were so young.

How I Became Battalion Mail Clerk

The last part of the flight to Vietnam was from Okinawa direct to Tan Son Nhut Airport outside of Saigon. The realization that we were in Vietnam hit all of us hard. I was out of high school less than a year, and descending fast as hell into a world I had watched on the news all through my last two years of high school.

We were rushed from the plane into an overcrowded, ancient terminal. Then, just as quickly, we were placed on buses and taken to our temporary housing to await assignment to a unit. From that first day, I had a sense that something wasn't right. I wondered why all the bus windows were protected by steel mesh. It made me feel more like a prisoner than a soldier. I was told that it was to protect us from the rocks that the locals had a habit of throwing at the buses.

My thought at the time was if they don't want us here what the hell are we doing here?

The compound where we arrived reminded me of the old western towns I had seen in the movies as a kid. A face I recognized from the airplane agreed with me. He introduced himself as Jesse James. I laughed and informed him that I was Billy the Kid. The names stuck throughout our short stay in the compound. I never did get Jesse's real name, nor saw him again. I hope he made it back to the world in one piece.

After the "Welcome to Vietnam" bullshit and assorted tips on how to survive your tour in Vietnam, I got the last good night's sleep I would have for a long time.

At roll call the next morning I was informed I was part of a group assigned to the 26th Logistic Division out of Da Nang. As names were called there was a rush to the map to see exactly where Da Nang was. The popular consensus was it was only halfway to the DMZ, so it couldn't be all that bad.

At a smaller compound in Da Nang, we went through the same welcomes and lectures again.

Another lousy meal, another night's sleep, and one more roll call for assignments.

At this point I look back at the training the Department of the Army gave me in preparation for my mission in the Republic of Vietnam. I would like to also point out the fact that I grew up in the city where I used public transportation to get around. I had never driven a car in my short, sweet life. The Army put me through basic infantry training, field medic school, and clerk typist school — nowhere was there a driving lesson.

The staff sergeant giving out the assignments was flying along. He simply matched MOS's (the job the army trained you for) with units that needed that skill. The concept made sense until it came to me. I was assigned to the 666th Transportation Company as a truck driver. I quickly slowed down the process. I informed the man that he had just made a mistake.

I went over my 201 file noting the following: I was trained in basic infantry at Fort Dix; medic training at Sam Houston; the art of typing and filing at Fort Polk. Nowhere had I trained to drive a truck!

Without a moment's hesitation the good sergeant reached behind his back to his collection of army regulations and cited one. It said: All 71B clerk typists can drive a one-quarter, and a three-quarter ton motor vehicle."

I was told that I could take the fact that I had never driven a car before in my life up with my new first sergeant. The staff sergeant yelled out, "Next!"

Once again I raced to the map to find out where my assignment was. The 666th Transportation Company was part of the 39th Transportation Battalion at Camp Eagle, the home of the 101st Airborne. I guess it could have been worse, I could have been sent further north into Quang Tri.

The trip to the Phu Bai airport, outside of Camp Eagle, was somewhat scary. As I sat bouncing around in the net seats listening to the hum of the propellers and trying my best not to throw up, I had one thought;

What the fuck am I doing on an airplane designed for jumping and heading for Camp Eagle?

We made it to Phu Bai in one piece. Our small group was directed to a small waiting area and told to "hang tight, someone will be along to claim you." It wasn't long before a truck pulled up and its driver shouted, "All aboard for Camp Eagle."

We tossed our shit into the back of the truck and began the last part of our journey. America already seemed long ago. We had been in the country less than a week.

As we drove through the outskirts of Phu Bai, the sight of a pile of bodies clad in black pajamas was my second taste of the war. As we closed in on Camp Eagle, the driver yelled out, "Any of you guys new drivers for triple six?"

He seemed happy to get a few "yows." He then kindly informed us that due to a lot of ambushes on the night convoys lately the unit was in desperate need of new drivers. I had a bad feeling in the pit of my stomach that the first sergeant was not going to be very happy when he found out that one of his new truck drivers had never driven anything in his life.

Camp Eagle was a large base which gave me a sense of security. My main concern was meeting the first sergeant. I will never forget my first meeting with Top. I was a twenty-year-old kid less than a year out of high school and scared shitless.

"What the fuck do you mean you do not know how to drive?" He gave no "Welcome to Vietnam" speech. He just leapt out from behind his desk yelling, "What the fuck is this?"

He ripped a beaded necklace from my neck. "When was the last time you shined your boots and had a haircut?" He went on. "Bright and early tomorrow you will be in front of this office with shined boots, a haircut, and you will learn to drive a deuce-and-a-half."

Before I had a chance to say anything, he turned and screamed to his desk clerk. "Get this fuckup out of my sight!"

I was in shock. Here I was in Vietnam and I had a wacked-out first sergeant who thought he was a drill sergeant and we were still in basic training. The company clerk took me to my living quarters — a small hooch with four cots, three rednecks, and a reel-to-reel stereo with hours and hours of good ol' boy country music. It was heaven if you like good old fashion country music — hell if you hated all forms of country music.

The company clerk told me not to worry about Top. Top treated everyone like shit. He gave me some downers, told me to have a few beers, and relax. I got real relaxed, threw up, and passed out.

Morning came fast. George Jones was still singing and my roommates were drinking their breakfast. Someone yelled to me to "get my shit together" and that Top was looking for me. As I got up, in somewhat of a daze, I heard the sound of crunching glass. As I reached down to pick up my smashed glasses I got quite a laugh.

Top was with the motor pool sergeant planning my day when I found him. I informed him that I could not see very well without my glasses.

The first sergeant calmly asked, "Where the fuck are your glasses?"

After showing him my broken glasses, I didn't get a word in. "Do you know how long it will take to get them fixed?"

All I heard after that was, "Get him the fuck away from me!"

The company clerk took me back to Hillbilly Heaven, and said, "Don't worry, Top will have a couple of shots of whiskey and settle down."

That was Friday and the first sergeant left me hanging through the weekend. Monday morning the company clerk came by and told me Top had called battalion head-quarters and given them hell. He told me that I had been transferred to Headquarters Company to fill a clerk job.

As he turned around to leave, he looked back with a smile and asked, "Did you break your glasses on purpose or did you just have a lucky day?"

I smiled and said nothing. By this time I could not get anyone to believe that it was an accident. I was just happy that I was spending my last night in the 666th Transportation Company.

I decided to spend that night enjoying a quiet movie. The movie was shown on a wooden screen down at the bottom of the hill. The "theater" had wooden benches going up the side of the hill. The projector was at the top of the hill in the NCO club. The movie hadn't been running very long when a loud explosion made me jump off the bench. I looked up to see half the crowd was calmly sitting watching the movie while the other half was looking up the hill and cheering.

I asked the obvious question. "What the fuck was that?"

The guy sitting next to me said, "Oh, that's Top's hooch. I hope they got the bastard this time!"

The next morning I woke early and was told to pack. My stay at the 666th Transportation Company was at an end. I was to report to Headquarters Company. As I was being driven to my new assignment I asked my driver how the first sergeant was doing. I was told the bastard was still alive.

I reported to my new job as a S-3 clerk with a sense of false security. I was beginning to believe that I was going to spend the war typing and filing away. This wonderful job lasted about a week.

I was filing some new regulations when I heard the warrant officer in charge screaming, "Who's reading this Communist literature?" He was holding my copy of *Rolling Stone*.

In a bad choice of words I said, "That's my personal property. Put it the fuck down!"

So much for that job.

It didn't take them long to find me a job no one was kicking down doors to get. Someone pointed out that the battalion mail clerk was rotating in two weeks. So I found a job I could handle. The following stories are based on what I saw and felt during my year as battalion mail clerk.

A Dialogue

Camp Eagle, July, 1970

Location: Spec 4 Whitehead's Barbershop

Spec 4 Whitehead: "I only do Afros and whitewalls." PFC Carney: "I'll go for the Afro."

PFC Carney (looking through magazines as Whitehead sharpens his straight razor): "It's quite a collection of *Jet Magazines* you have here."

Spec 4 Whitehead (smiling as he continues to sharpen razor): "You got something against *Jet Magazine*?"

PFC Carney: "No, they all have a fine center-fold picture."

Spec 4 Whitehead: "Grab a magazine and sit down. I'll be right with you."

PFC Carney (sits down, smiling he checks out center picture of a scantily clad beauty): "Take your time. I have three-hundred-sixty days."

Spec 4 Whitehead (as he ties a cloth somewhat tightly around the PFC's neck): "You like black women?"

PFC Carney: "A beautiful woman is a beautiful woman,

no matter what the color of her skin. Same goes for an ugly woman."

Spec 4 Whitehead: "You didn't answer my question."

PFC Carney: "Yes, I did. I like black women just as long as they're not ugly."

Spec 4 Whitehead: "I like white woman even if they're ugly. Would you mind if I dated your sister?"

PFC Carney: "I wouldn't mind if my sister didn't mind."

Spec 4 Whitehead: "Most white guys get upset when I ask that question. I can tell from their manner if they're lying."

PFC Carney: "That's interesting. Am I lying?"

Spec 4 Whitehead: "No, you're not even sweating. Racist tend to break into a cold sweat when I get behind them with a straight razor."

PFC Carney: "I don't blame them."

Spec 4 Whitehead: "I've had white guys tell me they would give up sex before they would have sex with a black woman. What do you think of that?"

PFC Carney: "They're fucking lying to themselves or they're lying to you."

Spec 4 Whitehead: "Ha ha! You want to take my bigot test?"

PFC Carney: "Do I really have any choice?"

Spec 4 Whitehead: "If you were at a party and Diahann Carroll and Kate Smith were coming on to you, which one would you fuck?"

PFC Carney: "That's the dumbest fucking question I have

ever been asked in my life. If anyone answered that question with Kate Smith, I wouldn't blame you for cutting their throat."

Spec 4 Whitehead (laughing loudly): "Whatever gave you the idea that I would ever do something like that?"

PFC Carney: "Diahann Carroll, has she ever posed for a *Jet* pictorial?"

Spec 4 Whitehead: "You pass my redneck bigot test. Do you want a haircut or do you want me to just swear to Top that I gave you one?"

Camp Eagle, August 1970

Speedy and Freddy Fender

The other day I heard an old familiar voice singing on the radio. It was Baldemar Huerta singing, *I Love My Rancho Grande*. Baldemar is better known as Freddy Fender these days. He is off the drugs and making a living with his unique brand of Tex-Mex music.

I remember the first time I heard Freddy Fender. I was picking up two replacements at the Phu Bai airport for delivery to Camp Eagle. I remember one of the new guys had this big shit-assed grin — the kind you just don't see on new guys in Vietnam. As a rule I would not introduce myself to the new guys. I would just tell them to jump in the back and promise to get them to their new home safe and sound.

Before I could say one word, the guy with the grin held out his hand and said, "Hi, my friends call me Speedy."

When he got settled in the back of the deuce-and-a-half, he asked if he could play some music. I said that it was fine with me just as long as it wasn't country music. I was about to find out that there was country music and then there was Tex-Mex music. I would not hear Baldemar sing in English until a few years after I got out of the service.

Speedy was assigned as a driver to the Battalion Headquarters Company so I saw him around a lot. I don't remember exactly when Speedy's smile disappeared — I guess it slowly faded away. I remember him telling me a couple hundred times or so that he never would do drugs again. It was funny; at times he seemed to be telling the picture of his wife and kids, "You can trust me. I'll never do drugs again."

It was about that time that rumors were flying all over the place. The word going around throughout Camp Eagle was that we were going into Laos or across the DMZ into North Vietnam.

If they were true, there sure as hell wasn't going to be any element of surprise for the Army of North Vietnam. It was around this time that Speedy's smile became just another stoned glare. Sleeping with his sunglasses on would be the first of many changes in his personality.

To this day I still do not understand how the United States court system and the United States Army could take a clean heroin addict and ship him halfway across the world to the heroin capital of the world. Vietnam in 1971 was the ultimate shooting gallery in more than one way! North Vietnam was pouring the little white powder down the Ho Chi Minh Trail just as fast as it was shipping weapons. Little vials of happiness for any G.I. that wanted to forget about the war for an hour or two. I know now that the thought of going home to San Antonio was not on Speedy's mind anymore. All he cared about was staying stoned.

The rumors turned out to be true. As usual the hooch maids and Popa Sans burning our shit knew more about what we were doing than we did. The news came quick.

We were ordered to pack up everything. The battalion was reassigned and we were leaving the relatively safety of Camp Eagle for the much more dangerous area of Quang Tri Province. It was during this trip that I learned the white powder had taken a friend away. As the convoy was preparing to pull out, I noticed Speedy throwing his shit on back of the five-ton I was riding shotgun on. The trip would take us through several small villages before we would get to our new home in Quang Tri. The outskirts of the villages, as usual, had their fair share of children begging and hustling food, or whatever they could steal from the back of the trucks.

As usual I had a few cases of old C-rations that I would trade for cold sodas from the kids on the side of the road. During a slowdown on the outskirts of one of these villages a kid, no more than ten years old, jumped on the truck and started throwing C-rations off. I thought what the fuck! I don't know anyone that eats that shit anyway. I know a lot of GIs that opened the Cs, took the cigarettes, and tossed the cans. It happened so fast that I'm not sure if I really would have shot Speedy or not. Speedy had grabbed the kid and was holding the kid's right hand down and was getting ready to cut it off.

Speedy was waving his Bowie knife and screaming, "I'll show you, fuck-an' gook. You can't steal my stuff."

I fired one shot a couple of inches over Speedy's head and told him he had two seconds to let the kid go or I would blow his fuck-n' head off. Speedy didn't hesitate. He let go of the kid fast.

I said, "Think of your own kid. If you weren't so fucked up on the coke, you would be passing the C's to the kid." It was the last time I saw Speedy's smile. He did not say a word. He just smiled as the convoy commander called me every name he could think up. The next two months were a horror show. I did not see much of Speedy during that time. It was back in Phu Bai that Speedy grabbed me from behind one day and threatened to cut my throat for stealing his drugs.

He screamed, "I know you took my dope."

I don't think he even knew who I was. He was not the same man. Coke makes you weak, thin, and slow. It was not too hard for me to get the knife away from him.

I got him to the medical unit, but the U.S. Army had a policy that said drug addiction was not an illness and they did nothing to help him. Vietnam had many ways to kill you. I could see how Speedy was going to die. I knew it was the only way he would ever find peace.

It was not too long after that incident that I was called to do a personal inventory of a soldier's belongings that had supposedly died from natural causes. As I packed that picture of Speedy's wife and kid, all I could think of was, *Why the fuck did they send a clean heroin addict to the big shooting gallery!*

Brother Love, Your Mother Is Calling

Some of us got so lost in the drugs and chaos of Vietnam that we forgot about the past as well as the people in it. Brother Love was one of those lost souls.

I could hear the Lieutenant Colonel screaming at the lieutenant who had been assigned as the Battalion Mail Officer. The screams echoed through the old wooden building. I knew instinctively whatever it was all about it was going to come my way.

Within seconds of the end of the screaming the lieutenant was in my face. It seemed there was one PFC Love who was not writing home to Mom and Mom was crying to the Red Cross. The Red Cross was crying to the Department of the Army, the Department of the Army was screaming to the USARV, and they were screaming to Division Headquarters, who in turn screamed to Battalion Headquarters. I was the bottom of Battalion Headquarters. Locate PFC Love and sit him down to write to Mom about the great time he was having here at Camp 'Nam! It didn't take long to tell the lieutenant to go fuck himself — I wasn't going to do his job. If he wanted PFC Love to write home he could go look for him. I had better things to do with my time.

Almost as quickly the lieutenant reminded me that my request for R & R at China Beach required his signature.

So began my quest for PFC Love and a letter to Mother Love.

PFC Love was in the 523rd Transportation Company and for a brief moment I considered passing the buck on to their company mail clerk. After giving it more thought I realized how nice an R & R at China Beach sounded. I decided to handle this myself, and contacted the 523rd's commanding officer explaining the situation.

The commanding officer of the 523rd Transportation Company informed me that PFC Love, as of his last Article 15, was Private Love. He directed me to the motor pool sergeant to track him down.

The captain gave me some bad news as I was going out the door — Private Love was a serious cokehead.

At the time I figured, what the fuck, everyone in the country was either a cokehead, a pothead, or a major fan of Jim Beam.

The motor pool sergeant's opinion of Mr. Love wasn't any better. He told me that he was part of a group of drivers that were running supplies from Da Nang to Quang Tri. The motor pool sergeant was your typical redneck. I asked him if he had any idea where Private Love was at the present time. He said, to the best of his knowledge, that he was AWOL somewhere in Da Nang. I asked him if he had informed the company commander of the fact.

"No," he said, "he might track the useless nigger down and bring him back. If he wants to kill himself with drugs, let him."

I said "so long" to one of the U.S. Army's finest and went on my way.

I was seeing my R & R slipping away as I explained the situation to the lieutenant. I got a smile and an order to include a trip to Division Headquarters in Da Nang as part of the next day's mail run. By the way if while in Da Nang I managed to track down Private Love and got a signed letter to his mother, he would find it in his heart to sign my R & R papers.

For a lot of people finding one missing cokehead in a city the size of Da Nang might be problem, but not for me. Now getting him to write a letter might be a hell of a lot harder. I told the lieutenant to call the motor pool sergeant and make sure he gave me the driver I requested for the next day's run.

I was at the motor pool bright and early the next morning with my request. When I told him I wanted any black driver that he thought did drugs assigned to the mail run, he gave me a funny look as he went for the phone.

If I wanted to find a brother with a coke habit, what better way than to get a brother with a coke habit for a driver!

The ride from Phu Bai to Da Nang was quick and safe — in fact it was a four-joint run. Just as soon as I took care of the mail and messages for Division, I asked my driver if he knew where I could score a couple vials of coke. His face lit up and I was on my way to Brother Love.

Before he tapped on the door of the hooch, he turned to me and said, "Be cool. Some brothers might not be too happy about seeing a white guy from Headquarters Company."

The hooch was a smoke-filled room with the sounds of the Four Tops overpowering any attempt at communication. As out of place as I was I think most of the people in the room were too stoned to notice anything.

It didn't take long for my driver to score. As I took the time to mix powder with some Salem tobacco I asked him if he knew Brother Love.

"That depends on why you want to know," he said.

I told him he had a big package from home that the company mail clerk had marked for return to sender, and I had heard that he was in Da Nang.

It wasn't long before I was introduced to Brother Love and asked if I was sent by the company commander to get him. With some assurance from my driver, Brother Love agreed to drive back with us to Camp Eagle as long as I didn't take him back to his company. I promised him that I wouldn't.

Brother Love slept all the way back to Camp Eagle. Once again we had a quick, safe trip. Taking into consideration my condition and that of my driver, that in itself was a miracle. I knew it would take another small miracle to get Brother Love to write a letter to his mother. When I got Brother Love to my hooch, he came back to the world. He had no idea where he was or how he got there.

As he got up to leave I explained to him why I brought him back to Camp Eagle.

He was not too concerned. As he said, "Fuck her, too," and got up to leave, I used the only thing I could think of to get him to stay — a vial of coke.

The next morning I was putting Brother Love's letter home in my mailbag as I prepared for my mail run. I asked Brother Love if he was going to write home on a regular basis or would I have to hunt him down every month or so?

As he walked away all he said was, "It doesn't mean nothing."

I never heard from Brother Love or his mother again. I don't know if he ever kicked the drug habit, or for that matter, if he ever even made it back to the world. Sometimes I wonder what he had to say about Vietnam in that letter.

S&S Staffer Finds

Just Flash a Sign 'You Want Heroin

By SPEC. 4 DAN EVANS
S&S Staff Correspondent

PHU BAI, Vietnam — I stepped out of the jeep at a market on the outskirts of Hue, and before I got 20 feet there were three men on motorcycles around me.

"You want girl, you want girl?" they chorused. "Number one girl, you go here," one said, patting the back of his cycle seat.

Squinting against the strong sunlight, I shaded my eyes and shook my head. My hand trembled slightly (purposely).

One of the 'cowboys' caught on. "You want coke?" He whispered. Another pulled out a vial of "cocaine." "You buy beaucoup, I souvenir beaucoup. You buy thi thi (a little), I souvenir thi thi," he said. "Souvenir" is slang for "give away."

Cocaine is rare in Vietnam and has never been found in northern I Military Region.

What pushers around Vietnam refer to as "coke" is really heroin, usually about 95 per cent pure. In the United States, heroin sold on the street has usually been cut until it is less than five per cent pure.

The cowboys were offering me heroin at $2 a vial. In the United States the same amount of "smack" would be worth about $100. And there it might be cut with strychnine, drain cleaner or worse.

The pushers wanted me to go with them. I told them that my friend would soon return for me. "Get the coke and come back here," I urged. They didn't buy the idea.

A U.S. 2½-ton truck roared by going north on the truck route through Hue. The GI on the passenger side flashed the peace sign and then crooked both fingers forward in a recognition sign of drug users in Vietnam. Two of the men on cycles buzzed off after the truck.

The third cowboy got down to business. He pulled a greasy, much fingered chunk of cardboard from his pocket. A GI had carefully block lettered a message on the card. It said the man's name was Kim. "He sells pure, uncut smack and he has the prettiest girls in Vietnam," the GI had written. A similar testimonial on the other side attested to Kim's trustworthiness. It was signed "Don."

Kim wanted me to go with him but I declined.

Finally he agreed to lead me and my friend to his source of supply.

My friend returned with the jeep but Kim didn't show.

One of the biggest heroin supply points north of Da Nang is Phu Long, on Highway 1 just north of Phu Bai and near Camp Eagle.

You can get anything at Phu Long, including being beaten and robbed or your watch ripped off. Such crimes are on the increase. Nearly nonexistent six months ago, armed robberies have jumped within the last two months, informed sources here said.

Anyone who travels extensively on the ground in Vietnam will find drugs available in most populated areas near U.S. troops.

Drugs in Phu Long are available everywhere. Just flash a peace sign, or put on a headband or sunglasses, or put one finger to the side of your nose as though you are sniffing "smack," and you will catch the eye of a pusher.

Ask anyone. If they don't have it, they probably know who does. Usually they are friendly—happy to oblige the buyer.

A kid selling ice cream sticks may have vials in his icebox. A woman squatting near the road may have hundreds of vials in her purse.

Later I stood along Highway 1 in Phu Bai with two cartons of marked American cigarets under my arm. A cowboy on a motorcycle pulled up. "You go to airport?" I asked.

He drove down the road and turned right, going past the joint U.S.-Vietnamese police station and toward the airport. Halfway there I asked, "You have coke?" He nodded violently.

He stopped abruptly and let me off short of the terminal. "You wait here," he said.

He turned around and sped back to the police station. He laid his bike down directly across the road from the station and dug in the grass of a vacant field. He stuck something in his pocket.

When he returned he carried a cigarette pack with several vials inside. I walked to the latrine directly across from the Phu Bai passenger terminal and he followed me inside.

He reached for the cigarettes but I said, "I want to taste." He handed me a vial, and I squatted beneath the window. I pulled off the cap and put my index finger in the white powder then put the finger to my tongue. It was stingingly bitter.

I looked around for an MP. There was none in sight. I stood up and spat on the floor. "Tastes like soap to me," I said. "Not mine," the pusher hissed. He knew that I knew that his "smack" was good. He took back the vial and ran toward his cycle.

I walked out of the latrine and into the terminal. There were a dozen men outside the building, and most of them stared at me. No one said . . .

Julius Hengele,
I Wish I Knew How To Spell Your Name

I can honestly say of all the people I knew in Vietnam, only one became a close friend. That was Julius H. from Philly. We first met the Monday morning I was assigned to Battalion Headquarter Company.

The hooch we lived in was broken down into small cubicles. His little world was across from mine. He introduced himself as Julius Hangelli (I never could pronounce it, yet alone spell it) from Philadelphia. He said he was the battalion draftsman. From the start I wondered what a transportation battalion did with a draftsman.

It didn't take me long to see why Julius was so important to the battalion commander. It was after about the third time I heard Jay (as he was better known) being dragged out of bed to meet with the battalion commander. Between the heat and my sudden need to know what the deal was, I decided to have a drink and sit up until Julius got back. It was a couple of hours later when he came back. He noticed that I was still up and poured a drink, and then he came in and sat on my cot.

I instantly asked, "What the fuck did the lieutenant

colonel need a draftsman in the middle of the night for?"

I got my first clue on how screwed up our battalion commander was with his explanation. It seemed the battalion commander was a speed freak that stayed up most nights planning his staff meetings. He had this big thing for charts. He counted his dead, his wounded, and the amount of losses on night convoys, the amount of losses on day convoys, the tonnage moved, the miles covered, and how many men were in the battalion that broke a toenail. You name it; he wanted a chart drafted for it.

Julius told me how he lucked into the job. He was trained to be a mechanic and was about to start in the motor pool when the lieutenant colonel checked his 201 file.

"The moment he saw I was a trained draftsman he had pictures of charts running through his head. Why do they even bother MOS with training?" he asked.

I related to that question. I soon learned that Julius and I had a lot in common — reading, drinking, smoking good joint, homemade spaghetti with a Rosie wine, and pretending that the war was just a state of mind.

I remember my first rocket attack. Julius and I grabbed our steel pots and flak jackets as we raced to the bunker. I looked into the bunker and saw a pair of green eyes glowing in the dark. You could hear the rats running around. I just freaked and bombed out of the bunker. Ever since I was a kid growing up in a project next to a dump in Boston, I've had this thing about rats.

From that day on whenever the alert went off Julius and I would just say what the fuck. We would light up a joint, mix a drink, and take our chances on a direct hit. Julius liked to check out the latest *Gentleman's Quarterly* and discuss fashions during rocket attacks. Throughout the first half of my tour I kept my sanity with conversations comparing Philadelphia to Boston.

Things were going too good. Rumors started circulating that we were going to be moving north. The rumors became fact as the 39th Transportation Battalion was quickly moved from Camp Eagle north to Quang Tri Province. Why we were moved north was still very vague.

My relatively safe job of picking up and delivering the mail and official documents a short distance was gone. What was more troublesome was the loss of my companionship with Julius. He stayed at battalion headquarters and I was forced to work out of a forward command HQ further north. At least he was safe and sound making grafts and charts for our insane leader. I was in a constant state of coming and going. Therefore I saw little of Julius. I was driving on Highway One and Nine every day, going back and forth between Vandergrift, Quang Tri, Phu Bai, and sometimes as far south as Da Nang. Combined with attachments of two Army companies, as well as two Marine companies, that made the breakdown and delivery of the mail more time consuming, I was somewhat overwhelmed.

It was in the middle of this confusion that Julius' tour came to an end. I never got to give him a hug and wish him luck back in the world.

We exchanged a couple of letters. I was caught up in a massive operation to finally close down the Ho Chi Minh trail. I guess Julius was caught up in the activities of the world.

Through the years I have thought of Julius and if I knew how to spell his last name I would have gone to Philadelphia to look him up. I don't think I would get too far looking for Julius, now would I? Well, Jay, if this book ever gets published and you pick it up, look me up. I live in New Hampshire, and I'm the same flibbertigibbet guy that I always was.

Jay in the corner of the photo, while the dogs play.
Camp Eagle, 1970

Some Things Are Better Off Forgotten
(Buried As Deep As Possible)

The Cathedral is a city within the city of Hue. It is protected by a city built around it, as well as its own walls. The North Vietnamese Army got through these walls and killed, maimed, and destroyed a beautiful city full of beautiful people.

Halfway between Quang Tri and the village of Phu Bai sat a French chapel built many years ago. Its last mission of hope was as an orphanage. One thing this war-torn country had was more than its fair share of orphans, and this little chapel was a crowded place.

I had heard it said that the hard-core North Vietnamese would cut off the arms from orphans eating food from the American soldiers. The North Vietnamese Army regulars would kill and maim children rather than allow American soldiers to clothe and feed them. This little old chapel had no walls around it, no city built around it, and no army within its walls ready to die defending it. All it had behind its walls where sad-eyed, lonely children incapable of understanding the hate inside the souls of the North Vietnamese Army.

That hate came one night, shortly after Christmas 1970. A hate that is better off forgotten buried deep in the parts of the brain that are locked tight.

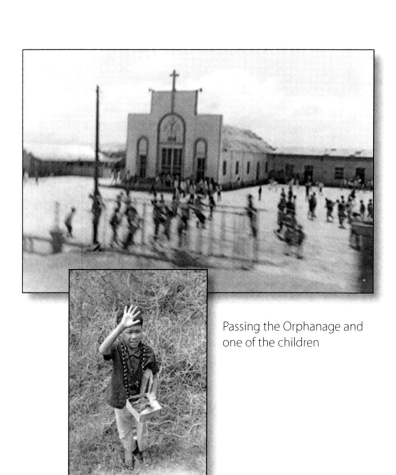

Passing the Orphanage and one of the children

Death on a Gun Truck

The sight of a five-ton truck, reinforced with steel panels, then armed with a couple M-60s and M-50s, is an awesome sight to behold for the first time. These trucks had names such as Dr. Doom, Uncle Meat, or The Assassin brazenly painted on their sides.

These trucks, with their four or five man crews, were intertwined in all convoys as the main protection against an ambush. Being the main offense during an ambush, they became the main target.

My job responsibilities prevented me from riding shot-gun on any of the many night convoys that took the brunt of these ambushes, but it didn't stop me from seeing the results of a bad night for a gun truck.

This story is somewhat of a quagmire. It's a look at how morbid we humans are. The quagmire is: am I being some-what of a morbid person for telling this story?

I don't remember the actual date that it happened. I do recall we were still in Quang Tri pushing supplies like cra-zy into fire bases along the Laos border. I had just pulled in from a run to Phu Bai and Da Nang as I noticed the staging area. Trucks were beginning to line up for what looked to be a large night convoy. I noticed the crew from one of the gun trucks that I knew from Camp Eagle, and I went over to shoot the shit.

It wasn't long before someone yelled to me, "Stop fuck-ing off and unload the mail."

With a smile I said "so long" realizing he had a point, and I went to break down the mail for the companies.

That night was like all the others since we moved to Quang Tri. I separated the mail by company, and then notified the company mail clerks that the mail was ready. After the last company had picked up and dropped off the outgoing mail, I smoked a joint or two, had a drink or two, and slipped into a semi-peaceful comma.

The next morning as I was loading the mail and preparing for my mail run, I got the news about the ambush. The word was that one of the gun trucks took a direct hit in the back. It was so bad that they were towing the gun truck in with the dead bodies still inside the truck. With a bad feeling, I set out to complete my run as fast as possible.

As I pulled in past the staging area, I saw the crowd around the burned out shell of the gun truck. I was about to find out how fucked up people are! I had a feeling no words can describe when I saw the name on the side of the truck. As I watched the crowd around the truck posing for and taking pictures, I thought I was going to throw up.

One of the vultures walking away with his camera in hand stopped to talk to me. He was kind enough to inform me that, "They were blown to pieces. They can't even figure out who's who."

The sick part is people were waiting in line to take a picture of the inside of the gun truck. To this day I still don't understand why anyone would take pictures of their own brothers in such a state. I just don't get it!

It was when the Triple Six company mail clerk came in to pick up his mail that I realized I had a problem. He was new to the job and he had not done personal inventories before. I knew starting off with four inventories was a little overwhelming and I offered to help him.

It was as though I had aged fifty years in the last few months. Here was this nineteen-year-old kid looking to me for answers on how to detach your personal feelings from your job. After all I was an old veteran and a wise twenty-year-old.

The Day I Almost Died

It's March 1993 in the middle of the night and I have just woken my wife with my nightmare. Some nights I pour a glass of whiskey, sit in the dark and remind myself where I am, and what year it is. An image of a burning truck and two mangled bodies are still as clear now as they were in the middle of March 1971.

In February of 1971, our unit was moved from Camp Eagle north to Quang Tri Province. From there we were relocated to Fire Base Vandergrift. My time in Vietnam up until this point was a picnic compared to the shit I was about to encounter. Death and fear were about to become part of every sunrise and sunset.

The days started early. With the heat of the morning sun I would begin my day with a joint and a beer, and then find my assigned driver. Next, as I sipped Kessler Whiskey (smooth as silk, so the label said), I loaded up the truck with the day's outgoing mail and battalion correspondence.

The nights were long and quite often loud. The first lesson learned was training your ears to know the difference between incoming and outgoing fire. In reality, unless you were drunk or stoned, night-time was no time to sleep.

In fact, the only night at Vandergrift that I recall sleeping through was when I was stone-cold deaf. The next day I went on sick call to have my ears realigned. To this day I have a constant ringing in my ears.

Back to the morning — the days all started the same at the fire base. After reporting to HQ that I was ready for the road, it was breakfast time. The constant buzzing of helicopters overhead seemed to merge with the morning heat. I usually sat on the side of a bunker to drink a cup of coffee and enjoy a continental breakfast. A good breakfast usually consisted of chipped beef on a bread product or powdered eggs cooked to perfection. It was impossible not to notice the huge Chinook helicopters overhead with their cargo nets loaded with dead ARVN soldiers.

The bodies of the dead ARVN's in the cargo nets of the big helicopters that died in the attempt to end the war on the battlefield of the Ho Chi Minh trail, were enough to make anyone sick to the bottom of their soul.

Little did any of us realize that we were putting our souls and lives on the line for nothing. As we toiled in the valley of death and eternal damnation, the dirty politics of Washington and Hanoi were, in fact, deciding the outcome of the war. After breakfast I would check to see if there were any special deliveries or pick-ups for Phu Bai or Da Nang. On the morning of March 11, 1971, my driver, the Monkey Man, Lucky Man, and I awaited word that the minesweepers had cleared Highway Nine. With the word we would find out if the minesweepers had missed any mines.

The Monkey Man with his monkey where on a mission to buy as much OB (a diet product bottled in France that consisted mostly of liquid speed) as possible. Lucky Man was rotating back to the world.

The most dangerous part of the day's journey was the ride along Route Nine east to Route One south. The road from Vandergrift to Highway One was long and curved, with its sides covered with tall elephant grass. A lot of the road had been hand sprayed with Agent Orange killing the elephant grass in an attempt to prevent ambushes. The curves led down through the "Rockpile," an area heavily infested with the enemy, and then through a few small villages before going into Quang Tri.

That morning, the all clear seemed to take longer than usual. My driver and I had a bad feeling. After one last joint, Monkey man, with an M-79, and Lucky man, with an extra M-16, jumped into the back of my truck. I put a couple of frags on my flak jacket, locked and loaded, and we started another trip through the "Rockpile."

The road seemed more curved than usual that morning, the elephant grass seemed taller, and closer even the sight of phantom jets off in the distance firing up areas of enemy sightings and ARVN patrols along the highway, gave me no sense of relief.

Lucky Man was rambling on about how so many guys got hit during their last week in country. The Monkey Man was stoned to the max talking to his monkey. I had my M-16 on my lap and was shooting the countryside up with my 35mm camera. As we took a sharp turn, I snapped a picture and then panicked.

I wasn't sure if the burning truck had been hit with a RPG round or had driven over a land mine. My driver quickly pulled the truck onto the side of the road as I emptied a clip into the elephant grass. Monkey Man and Lucky Man smartly lay low in the back of the truck to avoid sniper fire.

When I noticed the bodies by the sides of the truck I

froze. I just stared at the bloody mangled bodies of the driver and the shotgun that had been blown out of the truck. My driver quickly brought me back to reality. If the truck had been hit with a RPG round we were in serious shit. Somewhere in the tall grass was a small portion the North Vietnamese Army. If the truck had hit a land mine their bad luck was our good luck. Either way, we had missed death by one truck.

There we were, four of the Army's best, staring into the elephant grass, waiting to come face to face the enemy. There were no heroes here, just four scared kids. I couldn't keep my eyes off the men lying beside the burning truck. I was looking for some sign of life. I could see the driver, both of his legs were blown off, he was lying on his stomach,

43

and his back was bloody. The shotgun rider was lying on his back, his left leg and right arm had been blown off.

I still don't know — was it seconds, minutes, hours? Should I have risked sniper fire to see if they were alive and tried some first aid? Should we have fired up the area before we were fired on? I remember one thought going through my head, I'll die before I will let Charlie try to get me to talk about the documents I am carrying. Monkey Man was losing it. I think he needed a fix. Lucky man was crying and screaming, "I knew I would never make it back to the world."

Seconds, minutes, or an hour later — I don't remember — my driver was screaming, "I see movement in the grass."

"Fuck!" I yelled. "Fire up the area, open up, showing them we had some fire power. The sound of a Dust-off medevac helicopter hovering overhead was like an angel arriving from the heavens.

As quickly as the burned-out truck was pulled over to the side of the road, my driver had started up our truck, fired up a joint, and had started screaming, "Let's get the fuck out of here." I remember Monkey Man and Lucky Man yelling at me to get my act together.

Was it a dream? Was it reality? Is it 1971 or 1993? Was it seconds, minutes, or hours out of my life? I still don't remember. I can see the burning truck and the bloody and mangled bodies just as clearly as if it happened yesterday.

I still wonder almost every day, Are they alive? Are they dead? Did I do the right thing or did I just save my own ass?

Some nights I still stare into the night and wonder.

The Vandergrift Happy Hour

Fire Base Vandergrift was a tiny fire base in the northwest corner of South Vietnam. It was closed down along with Khe Sanh after the Marines survived a 77-day siege in 1968. In the early days of February, 1971, plans were put into motion to turn that deserted and barren area of Vietnam into another battlefield. A sign was posted less than two hundred yards from the Laos border: No American troops allowed beyond this point.

The real job of fighting back against the North Vietnamese in Laos was left to the South Vietnam Army. By the second week in February there were 20,000 ARVN troops massed along the Laos border. My transportation battalion was part of the 9,000 American troops that could only sit on their asses doing nothing.

For years the North Vietnamese Army had regrouped in Laos, getting well-needed rest as well as new supplies of Russian-made weapons. The war policy made in Washington, D.C. was that it would be bad manners to chase the enemy across the border. Being a well-mannered U.S. Army, we were ordered to stop at the Laos border.

Needless to say the American troops which supported

this massive offensive against the Communist Army of North Vietnam had, for the first time, something to die for. The fact that the Ho Chi Minh Trail was about to be shut down was, at last, a victory for the good guys.

From the first day an American soldier died in the defense of the Republic of South Vietnam, the Communist insurgents used Laos as if they owned it and the U.S. Government acted as if the world would end if an American soldier stepped foot in Laos.

The Communist insurgents from North Vietnam had started using the many paths and trails in Laos for supplies as far back as 1957–58. It was during that time period that President Eisenhower promised to support the government of South Vietnam against Communist aggression. Half-assed attempts to keep the promise were made by Presidents Kennedy, Johnson, and Nixon, as well as what seemed to be an endless supply of young men, some believing in a purpose, and some not so sure, to serve their country.

As the war lingered on thousands of young Americans died from the weapons that poured down the Ho Chi Minh Trail which all the B-52 raids in the world could not destroy. During this time period, presidents and presidential want-to-bes refused to see Laos as a factor in the war against North Vietnam.

My opinion is that in 1971, President Nixon was more concerned with his re-election than anything else on the planet. He became overly concerned with the liberal Democrats protesting the war, than with the soldiers in Vietnam and their families. He also forgot about the Republicans that supported his war position.

As President Nixon spent his days and nights with his

re-election worries, the ground rules of the most important battle of the war were drawn and played out. One has to wonder how General Eisenhower would have done during World War II with the rules of war the soldiers of Vietnam were stuck with. What if General Eisenhower was told he had no right to bring his army into France just because the German Army had the bad manners to invade it?

Just because North Vietnam was going in and out of Laos, that did not give us the right to go into Laos. This was the thinking in Washington throughout the war in Vietnam. The U.S. Army was forced to sit and watch as the North Vietnamese Army used Laos as an area for rest and to get resupplied.

While the Nixon administration spent all its time on his political concerns, General Abrams and the military command in Saigon finally took charge. The results of this operation and the comments made by our leaders clearly show why America lost a war for the first time!

In 1971, the leader of the Democrats, Mr. George Mc-Govern, blasted the administration for allowing the U.S. command in Saigon to put on a news embargo. For a change in war strategy, the U.S. command had hoped to surprise the enemy. In Vientiane, the capital of Laos, the Laotian Premier said he was opposed to any foreign intervention.

After years of looking the other way as the People's Republic of Vietnam used their country for their supply lines south, suddenly the Laotian government was concerned that the Republic of South Vietnam was taking short visits into their beautiful jungles.

The orders from Washington were still the same: no

American troops were allowed to enter Laos. At the same time the Paris peace talks were taking place. Kissinger, then Secretary of State, was seeking "an honorable" end to the war. Mr. Kissinger was promising to pull out. In short I was participating in a war that was over, which in some peoples' eyes never started. At this point in time, February 25, 1971, my life or death meant nothing. Washington had declared the war over for American troops, and was looking for a way out without destroying President Nixon's political career.

In Hanoi, the leaders of North Vietnam were pouring troops and supplies down the Ho Chi Minh Trail in preparation of their plan to take over the government of South Vietnam by force. All they were waiting for was the day the last American combat unit left South Vietnamese soil. Looking back on the situation, I am sure my life or death was of no concern to the powers in Washington or Hanoi. American troops in Vietnam in 1971 were not fighting a war. We had become a pawn between two governments. The good part was the government of North Vietnam had won the war over the Paris peace talk table, and not over my dead body.

In fact, as the Army of the Republic of South Vietnam was losing the battle over the Ho Chi Minh Trail, the decision was made in Washington not to bring in any American combat troops to insure a victory. The last defense to be used in the advent that the North Vietnamese Army decided to overrun Vandergrift was a massive B-52 raid. If your ass was in a bunker built by proper Department of the Army regulations, in theory you could survive a B-52 raid. As far as any other soul was concerned it was the "kill them all and let God sort them out" mentality that made

Vietnam such a wonderful experience. Anyway, back to my story.

Whenever the subject of the war comes up I tend to forget what year I'm in and my mind just wanders off. Now that you know where Vandergrift was maybe you can understand the story more.

By the middle of March, 1971, I was settled in to a deep, mud-filled bunker on Fire Base Vandergrift. I had adapted to the constant incoming and outgoing artillery barges. I had my ear canals flushed out, and despite a constant ringing in my ears, I could hear fairly well. I had my mail run down pat. I would always try to be the first truck out in the morning and the first truck back before nightfall. I would carry mail messages, orders, replacements, in general whatever or whoever needed transportation between Vandergrift, Quang Tri, Phu Bai, and sometimes Da Nang.

My ambition with every sunrise was to be back to Vandergrift by sundown. It seemed I had something in common with the enemy: they seemed to time their daily barrage with my return. I remember one day I had just pulled into the base and was about to unload, as the Vandergrift happy hour begun. I heard a whistle overhead, the next thing I remember was sitting in a bunker shaking dirt and debris out of my hair. Someone suggested I wait awhile before I attempt to unload the truck. I sat down and smoked a joint or two as a few more rockets came in.

I was getting somewhat thirsty and remembered the bottle of wine on ice in my bunker. It seemed like it had been quiet for a long time as we looked at each other to see who was going out of the bunker first. There was always a lull in between rockets and it was a tough call to make when the happy hour was over. By this time my throat was quite dry, and a cold glass of wine was looking good. The bunker I was in was about sixty feet from my usual bunker. I decided to go for it. I was about half way to my bunker when I heard the whistle over my head. I dove into the mud and crawled the rest of the way to my bunker. At the time a bottle of wine was about good a reason as any to die for. If you got anything from this story at all, you will know where I am coming from.

You already know my life or death meant nothing, so what if one crazy American Soldier died for a bottle of wine in Vietnam. I do not believe anyone would have given a shit!

Vandergrift Firebase

My Twenty-First Birthday

I had no plan of going AWOL, it just turned out that way. February 25, 1971 I did my mail run from Quang Tri, to Da Nang then back to Phu Bi only instead of heading back to Quang tri, I stopped on Camp Eagle. Frenche, our supply sergeant from New Orleans insisted that I partake of substance in celebration of my turning 21. I decided to stay one night, to sleep in peace and quiet on a real mattress with a pillow. I radioed to HQ that I had a flat but was secure with the mail and all correspondence on Camp Eagle. It would just be a 24-hour delay. The next day I picked up more mail checked in with Division then went back to Camp Eagle. I was twenty-one now. I was legally an adult. I now could vote against all fuck-head politicians supporting the war. I could now legally drink — as opposed to the illegal drinking of alcohol that I had been doing.

I had no plan of being AWOL for a second day, I was ready to head back north, but I lost my truck full of mail. It was gone? I smoked some weed, had a drink and sat listening to Country Joe and the Fish pondering my situation. The sound of a deuce-and-a-half pulling up sent me to the door, there was Frenche stepping out of my truck, with a big grin. "Where I come from, a twenty-first birthday party lasts more than one day," he said holding a big bag of weed. My driver looked at Frenche, then me, and said, "I will radio HQ that we are still working on the flat tire."

On the morning of February 27, the Sergent Major stormed into my hooch, dragged me off my comfortable mattress and almost soft pillow. He said Happy Birthday, and if I get the mail and all the correspondence from Division HQ up to Quang Tri before he got back that I would not be facing AWOL charges. I was a man now, my boyhood days were over.

Shortly my driver and I were back on the road heading North on Highway One.

Forward command HQ at Quang Tri

Rest and Relaxation

I never expected my request for R & R to be approved. I had requested an out-of-country R & R back in January for Sydney, Australia. I was sure it would be denied because of the ongoing operation in Laos.

The first thought I had was to find someone who could take over my mail run for a week. My trip to the land of round-eyed girls would be squashed unless I found someone with the clearance to pick up mail and dispatches from Division Headquarters. When we set up the Forward Battalion Headquarters, my alternate battalion mail clerk was left on Camp Eagle. He was about to have a rude awakening.

The next morning I kicked my R & R ticket out of bed. "Pack your duffel bag, the party's over. You are heading north!" I informed him. The kid was thrilled that he was getting to go where the action was. I knew then that I had my vacation from the war in the bag. I had been in-country for 252 days and now my mind was completely filled with thoughts of real world luxuries. My main goal was to have sex with a girl who weighed more than seventy pounds and spoke English!

My one-week replacement was too eager for me. This

scared me. My deepest fear was getting the kid killed so I could have a week of pleasure. I told him, "Don't do your own driving. Get an assigned driver from the motor pool every morning. As a rule, ignore what you have been told. There is no such thing as a friendly zone along Highway One. Shoot first, ask questions later. The life you save may be your own." The kid seemed to like the shoot first part!

After packing my two new suits, I was on my way to Cam Ranh Bay and a flight to Sydney. I have no words to describe the emotions that flowed through my soul as that plane lifted into the sky. A seven-day vacation from the war! It was like experiencing a miracle.

As we circled Sydney Harbor I had a dream-like feeling of landing at the airport in Boston Harbor.

Day One:

My first day in Sydney was spent in absolute fear. The bus drive to the R & R center was like driving through the Back Bay of Boston. Wow! I thought I could live there for the rest of my life. It was like the staff sergeant who greeted us had been reading my mind. The first words out of his mouth were, "I know some of you are thinking about deserting. It would be a big mistake! Any bad time incurred here will be added on to your in-country tour. Believe me you will be found, detained, and returned to the Republic of South Vietnam."

We were then turned over to the R & R center, and given local information.

I spent my first safe day pigging out on real food and drinking a vast amount of alcohol. I remained in the hotel, afraid to go out among civilized people! I just sat in front of the television, overwhelmed with the reality of my freedom.

Day Two:

On the second day of my trip back to civilization, I ventured out into the city of Sydney. I ate at a Kentucky Fried Chicken and wandered through a Woolworth's Five and Dime. For a short time I felt normal. I even had that familiar feeling I often had during walks through the streets of downtown Boston. Feeling comfortable that night I dressed up to go out to a "Whiskey-A-Go-Go" for a night of music and dancing. I realize how out of place I must have looked that night. The music was just loud noise, the flashing lights became flares warning me of danger! I wondered if my alternate mail clerk had got blown away so I could have this moment of freedom! I wondered if he was dying somewhere on Highway One so I could have this moment of living!

Out of the crowd came a real, live blonde heading in my direction. A blue-eyed, English-speaking girl came right up to me and asked if I would dance with her. It was not long before we were in my hotel room. She wasted no time in asking for money, saying she would spend the night with me. As we sat on the bed and made out, she suggested I go get something to eat while she took a shower. Being somewhat naive, I raced out for a bucket of chicken.

You guessed it right! I came back to an empty room — a very empty room. I did the logical thing; I went back out for beer and whiskey to go with my bucket of chicken.

Day Three:

Day three of my R & R was a hazy waste of booze and television. I recall getting dressed that night to go back to the Whiskey-A-Go-Go to find the bitch that ripped me off. I never got out of the hotel room.

Day Four:

Around noon, I decided to get dressed and go visit a local museum. One of my favorite places in Boston was the Museum of Fine Arts. I wandered around and was quite relaxed. Feeling hungry, I searched for a cafeteria. All was well until I got up to the cashier, who was staring at my neck. It dawned on me that I was wearing an AK-47 round on a chain around my neck. She started screaming about Americans and their war. "Why couldn't you at least have the decency to leave your bullets in Vietnam!" she screamed.

"Fuck you, too!" I screamed back.

The next thing I remember is being back in the hotel room drinking again. Day four of my vacation had me praying that the kid was not dying on my Highway One route. I thought about reporting back to the R & R center to go back to Vandergrift where I belonged. Somehow I ended up in a huge park, similar to the Boston Public Gardens.

I met another American on R & R, and a local girl he had befriended. We spent the rest of the day touring the beautiful city of Sydney. That night I planned once again to go back to the club to find the bitch that ripped me off. My new friend talked me out of it. We combined our funds to pay for two more nights in the hotel. We got shit-faced that night and talked all night about what we were going to do when we got back to the world.

Day Five:

The next day we made the mistake of turning on the news. A fire base along the Laos border had been overrun! A massive rocket and ground attack had devastated the base. I found out to my horror that my new friend was on R & R from Mary Ann, the fire base they had just informed us about. Outside of stocking up on booze and fried chicken, we spent the night in the hotel room. That night we shared our thoughts on going back to Vietnam and the possibility of never returning to America. We both knew in our hearts that it never would be the same. Neither one of us, at that moment, felt saving South Vietnam from North Vietnam was worth dying for.

Day Six:

I had decided my vacation as over. I packed my suitcase and drank as much whiskey as humanly possible. I reported back to the R & R center quite intoxicated, trying to keep the thought that someone may have died in my place out of my head.

My friend had left to meet his new girlfriend. He had made his mind up that South Vietnam's freedom was not worth dying for.

He went looking for a new life far away from Vietnam, and far away from America. The last thing he said to me was, "God saved me from Vietnam, and only the devil could get me to go back!"

April 11, 1971, Easter Sunday
from The Shores of Oblivion

It was in early December that I first met the chaplain and it was a rocky meeting to begin with. He demanded a salute and made a rude comment about my general appearance. I was facing one of life's great contradictions: a man of God who was also a career military man. After a Christmas Mass, I had asked him a question on that contradiction, he gave no real response.

It was in February when I had my second encounter with the chaplain. He was in a much better mood when he informed me that he was planning a trip to some of the fire bases up north. It was at this point that I could see the fear in his eyes at the thought of leaving the comfort and safety of Camp Eagle.

I said, "That's pisser. By next Christmas we'll both either be dead or back in the world." I had hoped at this point that I would not have to deal with him again. Sadly I was mistaken.

By the end of March, I was working out of Fire Base Vandergrift with companies of the 5th Transportation Battalion attached to my unit. I was handling twice as much mail, as well as other duties, plus driving longer distances on more dangerous roads.

It was April Fool's Day when the holy rollers asked me if the Chaplin would come to Vandergrift for an Easter Sunday Mass. All I could say was unless the Chaplin has changed his policy of staying on Camp Eagle the last few months, or if Chaplain Chicken Shit had been replaced, there was no way.

The fear of dying affects people in many ways. The look in these guys' eyes showed an Irish Catholic fear, the fear of dying with no last rites. In a way, it was that fear I saw in the chaplain's eyes at the thought of coming north to the war. It was not one of my better decisions, but I made my mind up the chaplain was going to give an Easter service that Easter Sunday on Fire Base Vandergrift.

The chaplain was about to see that I was a changed man. I believe once a man loses his fear of dying there is nothing you can threaten him with. At this point in time I had reached that point, and no matter what the Army would do to me it did not matter.

We were going to have an Easter Mass and maybe even have an Easter egg hunt. We could substitute the eggs with fragmentation grenades.

It was the same chaplain and he had the same song and dance. He threatened me with a court martial if I did not show proper respect for his rank. I found this somewhat amusing as I ordered the chaplain's assistant to respect my rank and pack whatever the good chaplain would need for an Easter Mass. Sometimes an M-16 can say for you what words cannot say. All I said to the man was, "Next Easter we will be back in the world laughing over this, or maybe we both will be dead and buried."

We left Camp Eagle and Phu Bai with a welcome for a new officer, orders, and the battalion mail. I was in a gracious mood and did not tell the new officer to go fuck himself when he pulled rank to sit up front. What I was concerned about was why the chaplain was not crying to the new guy about the situation and the fact that we were running late. Driving Highway One and Highway Nine in the dark was not a very bright idea. As I sat across from the chaplain, I passed him my rifle to hold as I lit up a joint. Seeing a look of total fear in his face, I assured him I hadn't lost anyone on the run yet.

From Phu Bai to Quang Tri is about a two-to-three hour ride if you don't hit a land mine, get hit with a round from an RPG, or take any sniper fire. My driver and I were aware of the situation, but the chaplain and the new guy were enjoying the beauty of the countryside. When we came around a curve on the winding dirt road a casuality of the war was lying on the ground.

My driver, having some common sense, went around the body and bike, and booked big time. I knocked the chaplain down under my body and got ready to rock and roll. Here is where it got strange. The fucking new guy put his foot on the brake and gave an order to go back to check on the health and welfare of the dead guy. I told the chaplain to lie down and not to move no matter what happened. The new officer was walking down Highway One without a weapon or a brain. I thought it wise to make him stop fast so I screamed out, "Get back here, shithead!"

It worked. As the captain raced to rip my lungs out, I saw an ammo box not too far away from the body and the bike. As my driver passed me a joint, he got ahold of the enraged new guy. As he pulled him behind the truck

I fired one shot at the ammo box. After the explosion, we were on our way.

The new officer was still pissed because I called him a shithead, but I left him with the thought that I would have let most officers straight out of OCS blow themselves to pieces. Anyway, all I had was one goal: To get the chaplain to give an Easter Mass. I quickly tried to assure him the rest of the trip would be safe and sound.

The chaplain, for the rest of the trip, tried his best to have a conversation with me. We even got down to a first name basis. I told him my friends called me Art, and asked him if chaplains had first names. It seemed Bob had a big fear of dying and was going through a crisis with his calling.

In a soft, almost tearful voice, he asked me, "How did you have the strength to risk your life for one Easter Mass?"

I didn't give it much thought at the time. I assured Bob that after his Easter Mass I would make sure he got back to Camp Eagle in one piece.

I did not attend the Mass. I spent that Easter Sunday inventorying the personal belongings of one Irish Catholic that never made it to his Easter Mass. I managed to have Chaplain Bob airlifted back to Camp Eagle early Monday morning before I started another trip south with a load of mail for the world.

Stand Down in Phu Bia

What happened after the great invasion is the heart and soul of what went wrong for the American soldier in Vietnam. For anyone who lived through World War II, I can explain it all in the next couple of paragraphs. For the rest of you it may be a bit harder to grasp. The Vietnam and Korean Wars, like WWII, had their final outcome depending on what the politicians in Washington, D.C. did. When Europe's struggle with fascism led to WWII, President Roosevelt didn't call it France's or England's war.

To equate President Nixon's war policy with President Roosevelt's, imagine it on the eve of the Jan. 25, 1945. President Roosevelt called Prime Minister Churchill and General De Gaulle to inform them that Americans have decided that no more Americans would die in Europe's war. Just picture President Roosevelt telling the people of France and England on the eve of the Norman invasion: "I am sorry, but for the rest of the war I can supply you with weapons, supplies and training, but no more soldiers."

That is exactly what we did to the Republic of Vietnam after Presidents Eisenhower, Kennedy, Johnson, and Nixon supplied troops to aid them from the invasion from the Socialist Republic of Vietnam backed by the Soviet Union. We plan the battle, but then we say you are on your own. The American people have decided that it's South Vietnam's war now. I still wonder what the majority of Americans would have thought if halfway through WWII our government turned its back on Europe, and said you are on you own from now on. Give that some thought.

The real change in American policy came when President Truman promised to support South Korea from the communist regime of North Korea and committed American forces. Not long after this commitment was made the Chinese communist forces invaded South Korea. When General Douglas MacArthur suggested invading China, he was fired. If he was president during World War II, would he have replaced General Eisenhower for suggesting invading France or Germany?

Back to Vietnam and President Nixon's leadership that led to the invasion of Laos and the Vietnamization of the war. We are into the heart and soul of what went wrong in Vietnam.

Patience was the key, that's what the North Vietnamese possessed and it is what we Americans had a total lack of. There was a sign over the headquarters of the 17th Cavalry that summed up the emotions of the American military in 1971: "Patience my ass. I want to kill something."

Throughout February and March of 1971, the 9,000 American support troops witnessing President Nixon's Vietnamization plan had great patience. We sat on our assess watching what should have been a great victory turn into a heavy defeat. What could have been, and for all practical purposes should have been, the greatest victory for the Republic of South Vietnam, turned into its gloomiest defeat.

The politics of the Nixon administration were a disgrace to all Americans. If his polices were used in the middle of World War II, we would of lost that war also. I have always wondered what side of World War II would such anti-war people as Abbie Hoffman, and Jane Fonda have been on. A major question I have of all those members of my generation that demanded peace at any price, would they have let Hitler take all of Europe while they lived in a dream world that he would never attack America? I am going to try to rope my ever-wandering mind in and get back to my story.

"Patience my ass I just want to kill something." By the end of May of 1971, I understood the meaning of that statement. Perhaps around the middle of April I was getting to that point. As the sun came up one April morning, I could see dark clouds of in the distance, a sure sign of the monsoon season. The sound of the Chinooks overhead was constant and their netted cargo of the dead from Laos was a gruesome sight. By now the invasion of Laos was turning into a disaster, and the ARVNs were in the middle of an ugly retreat. Most of the helicopter pilots I know were in a limbo, somewhere in between death and living. The final decision from our Commander-in-Chief was to let victory slip through our hands.

American pilots attempting to save their counterparts shot down over Laos were ordered not to land in Laos to save them! The Saigon command had direct orders from President Nixon, our Commander-in-Chief, not to bring up any combat units in support of the ARVN units in Laos. In short, President Nixon was waving a white flag to

Hanoi, and it was damn close to being over my dead body. The previous night's trip back to Vandergrift had been the longest it had ever taken me, and news from Division Headquarters was all bad. There were no orders to shut down the fire bases along the Laos border. The plan was to keep them open in order to give as much aid as possible to the retreating ARVNs.

The number one concern for the transportation units was to salvage or destroy any equipment and supplies that were about to fall into the hands of the North Vietnamese Army. The last couple of weeks I had seen Highways Nine and One turn into a massive movement south. It seemed the whole population of Quang Tri Province was heading south. As I took the turn west on Highway Nine I couldn't tell the heavy dark rain clouds from the thick dark smoke that covered the sky. A burned-out rubble replaced what had been a quiet little, lively village just twenty-four hours ago.

Last night was a long night of chaos and confusion. With the help of a drugs I was close to going into my fifty-some-thing hour without sleep. The darkness lead to the usual exchange of fire and another night of wondering if this was the night we would be overrun. No major ground attack occurred, just a very well-planned sapper attack. Under the cover of the night a small team of the NVA walked or crawled through our defenses into our main communication center, and blew it up. Our battalion commander jumped on top of a flatbed screaming for the troops to rally around him. Amazingly no one took a shot at the uninspiring bastard. The morning sun was coming up as I smoked a joint in an attempt to come down and prepare for another mail run.

I was picking up the mail from Headquarters when I heard the commotion. It sounded like one hell of a staff meeting. As a junior NCO, I felt obligated to check it out.

As it turned out it was the most emotional gathering of officers and NCOs I had ever witnessed. A decision was made Fire Base Vandergrift had served its purpose and it was time to try to get out alive! Being the nice guy I am, I brought it upon myself to pass news of the decision on. It was a great close-out sale for the NVA, and they quickly gathered up every piece of usable supplies left behind. The NVA plowed a road from the DMZ down through the chain of fire bases along the Laos border. In the long run, they probably got more supplies from these bases than was destroyed in Laos. In reality, this was the day America lost its first war. The North Vietnamese Army was now crossing in and out of Laos as it pleased. They had even gotten a bonus as Quang Tri Province was being cut in half.

The Nixon administration did the honorable thing and would not allow its soldiers to set foot in Laos. It never let them cross over the DMZ into North Vietnam. All these years, all these dead Americans, all of this was for one final day of retreat. So there we were, what was left of the 39th Transportation on its way back to Phu Bai with nothing to do but drink, do dope, and play with our toys. Even before we returned to Phu Bai it was obvious that things were getting a little insane. In the last month or so a lot of strange things had happened in Quang Tri Province making it even harder to know who the enemy was.

Things had gone insane even by Vietnam standards. Shortly before we had returned to Phu Bai, one of the 666th company truck drivers walked into the Quang Tri mess hall, shot his CO, and then blew his own head off. A new officer was wasted after forcing his way into a hooch and demanded that it's inhabits turn their music off.

The strangest of all these insane acts was the shooting of MPs on Highway One. Some real sick puppy had decided to set up speed traps to slow down the trucks on Highway One. I know one shotgun that had an ugly dispute over the matter. I mean, slowing down the traffic to protect the water buffalo was nice, but for some of us we were wondering if the water buffaloes were cover for snipers.

By the end of April, 1971, my state of mind was somewhat screwed up. I kept on having dreams of going back to high school after my last seventy-two days here in never-never land. I had my own little mail room with my private living quarters in the back. I had all the sour mash you could drink, all the grass you could smoke, and still I was not happy. I lived in a constant fear of what was going to go wrong.

I was spending most of my time alone pretending a battalion mail clerk's job was a lot more time consuming than it was in reality. I was up and out on my mail run long before I really had to be just to avoid the shit going on. Formations, roll calls, and inspections where making a comeback. Painting, sandbagging, and endless details in the motor pools became the major events of the day. Most of the people I was remotely close to were either dead or had rotated back to the world.

Wayne, a communication specialist, was just about the only member of the company that went back to my early days at Camp Eagle. I would spend most of my nights with him and his collie in the communication bunker. The dog had actually been in the Headquarters Company longer than anyone could remember, having been with us on

Camp Eagle, Quang Tri, Vandergrift, and now in Phu Bai.

There had been some tension between Wayne and the Monkey Man since we had gotten back from Vandergrift. The Monkey Man had brought his pet back to Phu Bai with him, and had been keeping it on a long chain in front of his hooch. The problem was Lassie liked playing with the monkey, but the monkey was scared shitless of the dog. In other circumstances the kids would have settled the matter in a more peaceful manner, but here in never-never land the boys took death a little too lightly.

The boys also had automatic weapons for toys!

Quiet nights were becoming the norm and I was getting used to them. One night I heard a burst of fire outside my hooch. I raced out of my hooch with my M-16 locked and loaded, and I saw the Monkey Man with an AK-47 in his hands. I didn't notice Lassie right away and was standing in kind of a daze when Wayne grabbed the weapon from my hands. It was at this point that I noticed the mangled body of the dog. I just managed to push the M-16 into the air as Wayne fired at the Monkey Man.

Lassie

By this time there were too many weapons, too much drugs, and two sides of a very emotional issue: lonely children and their pets. For all the bullshit and macho garbage, all we were was kids who loved their pets. In all the confusion and anger no one was shot, but for all we had gone through it was the first time I saw Wayne cry. The sad fact is we had reached a point of accepting people killing each other, but killing monkeys and dogs was going too far.

My last days in Vietnam where getting a little too shaky. After this incident a policy of keeping the weapons locked up was started. I was not eager to give up my M-16. Luckily the armory sergeant didn't like the idea of getting up at the crack of dawn to sign me out a weapon. Maybe it was the thought of pissing of the battalion mail clerk, either way I was allowed to keep my weapon locked up in the mail room.

I was closing in on June; my last full month in Vietnam, and the battalion was building up for a new operation in the A Shau Valley. The latest rumors had the transportation unit assisting the ARVNs in sweeping some NVA out of the valley. I was too short for any of that shit and prayed that I was long gone before the operation was put into action.

I had no desire to be a sacrificial lamb for Washington's tomfoolery — to fight the war or not to fight the war. I had been in Vietnam close to a year and the gutless politicians in Washington were still debating the issue. The question never was answered, just put on everlasting hold as the war started, was fought, then ended.

Somewhere in this mess is a story. I was lying on my cot one night in June of 1971. It was around midnight, but I was not sleeping. I was thinking about the world in a semi-conscience state and basking in the glow that the war was one day closer to being over for me. I heard Wayne banging on my door telling me to get my M-16 and come with him.

We went back to the communication bunker together. Wayne was extremely close to losing it all together. He had picked up screaming and yelling over the radio. I could hear screaming, "They're coming through the wire," and small arms fire. I asked Wayne if he notified the officer in charge. He said he had, and was told not to worry about it.

"If it advances to our perimeter, the perimeter guards would sound the alert." He would not bother the CO or the armory sergeant unless the perimeter defenses sounded an alert.

It was to be the last night I would spend in the communication bunker with Wayne. With my M-16 locked and loaded we made plans for after the war. As a sense of security came with the light of day, he went off to sleep and I went off on one of my last mail runs.

Monkey Man's monkey in front of his hooch

Good-Bye ACE

There is no doubt in my mind that Lieutenant Colonel Alvin C. Ellis, Commander of the 39th Transportation Battalion had more of an impact on me than anyone I served with, or under, in Vietnam. It was a strained relationship from the first day I met him up until the day his helicopter took off after a change of command ceremony in June of 1971.

In the eleven months that I knew and served under his command I never got a clue of any views he had on our reasons for being in Vietnam. I recall his first impact on my tour. I confronted the Warrant Officer in charge of S-3 over why he was so upset about finding a copy of *Rolling Stone* on my desk. He said he couldn't care less about what I read, but the Battalion Commander had a different viewpoint. "Dickhead feels that anyone reading *Rolling Stone* is a pot head and he feels S-3 is no place for a pot head. He went on to say, "No one argues with ACE no matter how right you are, you lose the argument."

By my third day in the Headquarters Company: My roommate had given me an insight to ACE's bizarre midnight staff meetings and his fascination for charts and graphs. By my fourth day I had my first personal run-in with the Battalion Commander. It seemed he felt that I did not give him a proper salute. I had a theory: If an officer wanted a salute he would give a salute first. If an officer did not want his rank noticed from a distance during war-time, he simply would walk by an enlisted man with a nod. No. Not ACE! He always expected an enlisted person to drop whatever they were doing, and let the fact that he was an officer be known by any sniper with a scope. I also found out that day that ACE had strong feeling about the relationship between officers and enlisted personnel. The Lieutenant who was the Battalion Postal Officer explained that the old man had strong feelings about officers being leaders and enlisted personnel being followers.

As he put it: "If there was not such a desperate need for someone to pass the test to be qualified to pick up the Battalion's mail and get a top secret clearance that I would be back with triple-six as their company mail clerk. Please honor the asshole with a salute." With that thought in mind I got a copy of the Army Post Office regulations regarding the duties of a battalion mail clerk and did some studying. I took their little test and I became the Battalion's mail clerk. From the start I had a sense that besides the real war there was also a class war and a cultural war going on within the Headquarters Company.

Up until early September I managed to avoid ACE, do my job and work on staying high. Then the package arrived. The package was addressed personal for Alvin C. Ellis and it had quite an odor. I personally placed the foul-smelling package on ACE's desk while he was out of his office. I was sorting mail for the companies when I heard the sound of ACE's lunch making a comeback. It was shortly after that

that I was informed the Lt. Col wanted to see me ASAP. I thought it smelled like a dead rat, but I really didn't think that anyone would mail a dead rat from the world, yet there was ACE screaming, "*WHAT THE FUCK IS THIS.*"

I said: "Looks like a dead rat to me, Sir."

I had even saluted him when I entered his office. This was the second of the many battles I would have with ACE concerning my job as Battalion Mail Clerk. He never did give me a chance to explain that under U.S. Army regulations I had no choice but to deliver the package. All I heard was "pack your shit you're going to a line company ASAP; get the fuck out of here!" I was packing my shit when the Battalion Executive Officer came in and told me to unpack. Since there was no alternate battalion mail clerk that he would be the only person that could pick up the battalion's mail, and he was not going to be stuck in that position. It was not until the next morning that he informed me that I still had my job. He strongly recommended I stay as far away as possible from ACE for a week or so.

It wasn't until October that Ace and I were once again in a talking relationship and it was not a friendly relationship.

It was in October when we clashed once again. I had let someone use the three-quarter assigned to me, to go to a local village to make an important purchase. It was a couple of hours later when they towed my truck in. The word going around was that I was hit by a sniper while I was on a carrier run. News traveled fast that someone else was driving my truck and that it was not an official run. Once again ACE and I had a difference of opinion on my performance as Battalion Mail Clerk. The issue was over unauthorized use of a government vehicle, and trying the screw that got shot.

He was being charged with being AWOL and being dishonorably discharged with loss of all benefits.

I was stuck; I could say that he took the vehicle without my permission or admit that I allowed him access. By the time the true story came out that the wounded soldier was shot in the hand by his own M-16 accidentally, I agreed for once with ACE that; the shithead was not going to get a purple heart and sent back to the world. I stated that he took my vehicle without my knowledge, and the issue died. I would not find out until months later that a Congressional investigation had over turned his dishonorable discharge.

Outside of pissing on his jeep whenever possible; I was blessed with not being in the presence of our commander up until November. A couple of weeks before Thanksgiving I noticed an unusual amount of supplies being delivered to ACE'S hooch. A week before Thanksgiving I found out what was going on. The Battalion Commander was planning a dinner complete with fine dinner china, and silverware for all the officers in his battalion. I am still not sure why it bothered me so much, but I was outraged at the time. The thought of their dinner and the enlisted men's dinner of frozen turkey breast, canned peas, instant potatoes, and powdered milk served on paper plates with plastic spoons and forks just did not seem right or even democratic to me then or now.

I guess from the moment that I found out about the dinner I made my mind up I was going to attend. It took a lot of banging and a strong push to see what I hoped I would not see. For that evening the officers were back in the world with their fancy dinner. It was the Sergeant Major, the highest rank in the enlisted ranks that opened the door. He was the only enlisted man in the room.

After a moment of eerie silence he quickly yelled, "He's a NCO and a member of Headquarters Company, make him a plate."

I could see the anger in ACE's face as he saw my face. The Sgt. Major quickly passed me a glass of wine, passed me a plate and hustled me out the door. Outside he looked me right in the eyes and said, "Sometimes for your own good you have to go along with things as they are."

This reminded me of my father who often said, "Sometimes you have to play Micky the Dunce." A reference to a "dumb Irishman." When I was a kid, I thought he was talking about Mickey Mouse. I said, "I can understand the Junior Officers sucking up, but not the army's highest-ranked enlisted man."

"You have all the rank you're ever going to get and you are a NCO, not a commissioned officer, act like one." He hesitated for a moment looked right in my eyes and said, "Son, I've been playing this game longer than you have been on this Earth, I know what I'm doing. Just be grateful I'm here. This will be forgotten in the morning. If I was not here and if I did not like you. MP's would be dragging your ass off for about six months of bad time for assaulting an officer."

I just tossed the plate and glass aside and walked away. The matter was never brought up again.

I made it all the way into the middle of December before I had anything to do with ACE. I was ordered to report to his office ASAP. I believe this was the only meeting we ever had that did not explode into a shouting match of threats. He had the log book from the motor pool that showed my mileage and gas use for the last thirty days. He quietly asked me why my mileage and gas use was not matching up with what the mail run should be. He also asked why I was taking supplies from the mess hall and other areas on my mail run? For the first time ACE was talking to me, not at me, and it felt fuck'n eerie. "I know you hate my guts and disagree with everything I say or do, but for once trust me. I know what I'm talking about. The VC do not like Americans feeding their children and poisoning their minds even if they are orphans."

All I said was, "It's my life and if I get killed feeding kids there it is."

ACE quietly replied: "I don't give a shit if you get your head blown off but I know the VC, I know how they think. They will take their revenge out on the children at the orphanage, not on you, for excepting the gifts."

For once I would find out that the Lieutenant Colonel could be right. It was about a week and a half before Christmas when Charlie showed me how strongly they felt about American Soldiers poisoning their children's minds. They would go so far as to cut off the hand that accepted food from the American's invading their country. ACE was right. Charlie did something much worse than putting a bullet through my brain, he left it intact with a working memory.

Throughout the rest of December and January it seemed every time I saw ACE he was walking in the other direction. It was not until February that we would talk again. As the Battalion Mail Clerk I was ordered to attend a briefing on an upcoming Division operation.

At this meeting, ACE wanted me to stop using assigned

drivers from the motor pool. He felt strongly that I should go back to one assigned driver or shotgun, whichever I preferred. I already had one driver I was close to get hit by a sniper, and I felt much better riding each day with whoever they drew from the motor pool. ACE was at his best as he put it, "Get your shit together. This is a transportation company in a combat zone and drivers get killed every day; accept that fact and do your fucking job. If you cannot do the job, pack your shit and I will get someone that can do your job."

Once again it was the Sgt. Major who interceded. After the meeting he pulled me aside. He told me as far as he was concerned the motor pool Sergeant has orders to assign me a driver from the motor pool as a priority each morning. That order will not be changed unless you request it. This was just before our move north and ACE knew my job was about to become much more complicated and a lot more dangerous.

I had been hanging out in the communication bunker listening to conversations from some on the convoy commanders and HQ, smoking, drinking playing a never ending game of monopoly wasting the nights away. One night I heard an in intense ongoing argument between ACE and a Convoy Commander. The convoy commander felt it was best to turn back the convoy of flatbeds carrying beer and soda. He was more than a little concerned over how high the river was they were about to cross. ACE disagreed and gave the convoy commander a direct order to have the convoy cross the bridge.

Shortly after a period of silence, we heard yelling and screaming as one of the flatbeds was washed over the side of the bridge. At this point everyone in the bunker agreed fragging the asshole was not such a bad idea! In fact it might increase all our chances of returning to the world in one piece. By this time there were a lot of people in the Battalion with the same thought.

The fact of the matter was ACE was like a phantom, no one ever knew where he was. He would pop up on convoys he would pop up in the middle of the night calling for a staff meeting. By February, we had moved to Quang Tri and had four additional companies. Two Army companies and two marine companies had been attached to the battalion. As usual ACE and I were in disagreement over the way things were being done. I was working the mail out of a mail room in the forward Command Headquarters in Quang Tri. I felt that I should have been sorting out the mail at night on Camp Eagle especially with the attached companies, and delivering the mail to the companies during the day. ACE disagreed, so I was forced to travel on Highway One from Quang Tri down to Phu Bai and back to Quang Tri to sort out and deliver mail from a makeshift mail room. Little did I think that it could ever get worse but, boy was I wrong.

In March we moved the forward Headquarters further northeast to Fire Base Vandergrift. Now I really believed ACE's main goal was to see me dead. I began driving my mail run from the Fire Base taking Highway Nine west to Hue then Highway One south to Phu Bia and back every day. Some days I would even have to go on to Da Nang then back to Fire Base Vandergrift. After that trip I would have to sort out the mail for the company clerks to pick up and drop off the next day's outgoing mail.

I would spend the rest of my time trying to keep up with my other duties that came with being the Battalion

Mail Clerk. I decided, once again, to discuss the issue with ACE. Once again I gave my viewpoint to the Lieutenant Colonel explaining that driving this distance on these roads every day, and running a battalion-size mail room with this many companies from the back of a trailer was downright dumb.

I should be running the mail room from the Battalion HQ on Camp Eagle and then deliver the mail to Quang Tri, Vandergrift, and line units by helicopter.

ACE listened quietly until I finished then let out a mouth full, "This is a transportation battalion I'm losing drivers every day transporting supplies, and you are no better than anyone else in this battalion. You're moving your mail by truck. It will be a cold day in hell before anyone in this Battalion will request any help from the airborne in transporting anything!"

I got the message, he had a point to prove and proving it over my dead body would not bother him in the least.

I never requested anything from the bastard again. I just got into a routine of starting my days with a joint and working on a steady high the rest of the day. Every day I made it back to Vandergrift in one piece. I felt blessed to be back in time for the daily rocket attack. I seldom saw ACE, but from what I heard his biggest problem was his own troops taking pot shots at him whenever he rode a convoy as the convoy commander. It was near the end of the invasion into Laos as the politics of Washington, Saigon, and Hanoi were turning the operation into a total disaster that I realized ACE had lost it completely. We had a long and powerful rocket attack followed by a well-organized sniper attack on the communication center. A clear threat of a massive ground attack existed.

Our orders from division was simply stay in your bunker until the last B-52 bombs were dropped on us was long gone. Anyone who paid attention to Division orders was aware of this fact but it looked like ACE never got the message. Our fearless leader, in the midst of all the confusion, jumps on top of a flatbed screaming out orders.

The only amazing thing is no one shot the stupid son-of-a-bitch on the spot. I guess no one really believed what they were seeing even for ACE this was one strange move.

It was shortly after this and a series of chaotic staff meetings, as well as some strangely indecisive orders from Division Headquarters that Vandergrift was deserted somewhat rapidly. We ended up back in Phu Bia on stand-down with ACE and his scrambled brains still in command.

By this time ACE and I were both short and we should have just counted our days in peace. This was not to be. ACE would stay ACE until the bitter end. His new challenge was to turn a Battalion of battle-weary men back into a bunch of scared kids fresh out of basic training.

It was during this disaster that I would have my last personal encounter with ACE. I had my own personal hooch as a mail room and my living quarters in the back. It was complete with a patio, lawn chairs, and a grill. It was early one beautiful June evening, and I was enjoying a steak and cocktails with a couple of friends when a rocket landed some were off in the distance. The alert went off. Everyone started screaming "*Incoming!*" The race for the bunkers was on. Flak jackets and steel pots were flying. We decided not to let the steaks burn, and to just watch the show. ACE, for some odd reason, was quite perturbed, and as soon as the alert was called off I was ordered to pack and move out of the mail room ASAP. Also, the Lieutenant Colonel desired to meet with me the first thing in the morning.

By this time I was very tired of ACE's stupid games and I reported to him the next day well-prepared. He quickly informed me that I was going to be replaced as Battalion Mail Clerk. I informed him that under U.S. Army regulations he would have to move the sergeant that he just moved into my old quarters, for the security of the U.S. Mails. He informed me that, "It was not My concern, that I no longer was a member of Headquarters Company. I was being reassigned back to the 666 Trans. Company."

He also said that their Company clerk was the new Battalion Mail Clerk. I informed him that he had no Mail Officer and no alternate mail clerk, and that if I was being replaced for not doing my job properly that I, in good conscience, could not train a new clerk. I gave him a copy of the Army regulation and said, "In fact, until someone passes the required test I'm the only person in the Battalion authorized to sign for the mail."

ACE just quietly stared off into space, turned to look at the calendar and said, "Get the fuck out of here, if we never see each other again, we will both be happy."

As June came to a close I waved good-bye to ACE as he climbed into a helicopter after a change of command ceremony. The only thing I regret is not seeing the look on his face as the sand on the helicopter pad was blowing away to show the peace sign we had painted as a good-bye gift for ACE. It was not as big as the one that the engineers made in Quang Tri. Still, it was nice.

I wandered into the small hooch designated as the enlisted men's club early on a hot September day. The drink of the day most days was rusty cans of fascia, a rusty can of Blue Ribbon, Lone Star beer, of a glass of Kessler, smooth as silk whiskey. On this day the keeper of the bar was wearing a yarmulke and serving a Manischewitz Concord Grape Wine. With a happy New Year prayer and a toast we sipped the grape. By the third glass it started to taste real good. By the third bottle we agreed that the war made no sense. Other people came and went ignoring our assessment of the war. The next day, the first day of the Jewish New Year, I had a horrible headache, and I still was in Vietnam in the middle of a senseless war, from my perspective.

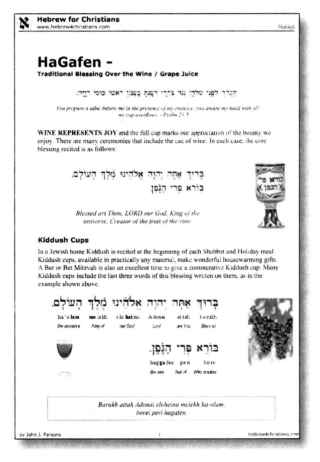

1971—Christmas/ Our New Year's Eve Then Their "Tet" New Year's Eve

Christmas brought us Bob Hope, and I share my thoughts on that later. It was an odd clear, quiet night that Christmas Eve. The bright stars in the night made me think of the night the Magi crossed the desert in search of baby Jesus. I made the latest possible mail run in search of last minute Christmas package from the World. I had received my Christmas wish, jars of spaghetti sauce, boxes of rigatoni and ziti and a jar of grated Parmesan cheese.

Also my wish for Christmas Day became a reality, no one died. The disturbing things in my box of Christmas goodies were pictures of my mother taken at an antiwar rally on the Bunker Hill Monument Park. I felt that my own mother was protesting against "me" joining Hanoi Jane. It would be years later before I got it. The Vietnam War never would have had an ending like Korea, had it not been for the massive amount of people in the streets calling for its end.

As for January 31st 1971, our New Year's Eve was quiet. Tet Nguyen Dan, the Vietnamese Lunar New Year, began on midnight January 27, 1971. It was the calendar year of the Hog. Compared to 1968 it was a picnic, we had a few rockets come it but no massive Tet attacks like those on 1968. This Tet, the South Vietnam Army with support troops from the U.S. Army was planning its own offense into Laos to shut down the Ho Chi Minh trail.

The Long, Lonely Trip Home

I spent my last night with the 39th Transportation Battalion in the communication bunker with a friend. Wayne was the last member of the Headquarters Company that I had any emotional attachment to. When his shift came to an end, I simply said goodnight. I went to bed and pretended to sleep. With the first ray of the sun I jumped up. I quickly threw my shit on the back of a deuce and a half, and waited for my driver. I was on my way to Cam Rahn Bay and my Freedom Bird.

Throughout the drive to Cam Rahn Bay, I had the same fears that all short-timers had: the fear of getting blown away on the last run; the fear of stepping on a mine on that last patrol; the fear of being shot down on that last bombing run; even the medics had the fear of being shot down on that last medical evacuation. There are no words to describe the feeling I had when we arrived safe and sound at Cam Rahn Bay — the home of the Freedom Bird.

After 364 days of serving God and Country in Vietnam, all I wanted to do was go home, go back to high school, and go back to being a teenager on the corner once again! Yet, I found myself once again in a barracks full of strangers waiting for their assignments — even though we all knew we were going home still we were strangers. Our feelings, my feelings were indescribable, when we, when I, arrived safe and sound at Cam Rahn Bay — the home of the Freedom Bird.

I looked for faces from the flight that brought me to Vietnam. All I could see were the spooked, tired, and empty faces of strangers. I thought that all they would do was check my orders, say thank you, and put me on a plane. It was not that fair and simple — like everything else in Vietnam, it was fucked up. First things first: a piss test was required, after all the Army did not want to send drug addicts back to the world. They did not want us to take home any things that might show America what the war in Vietnam was really like.

No pictures that did not show a smiling face and no contraband (any proof that the North Vietnamese Army existed). No souvenirs, no brass, no weapons, and no drugs not even in your bloodstream. Right away, I knew I would have at least a twenty-four-hour delay. I quickly became convinced that the delay would lead to death. It was a strange, eerie feeling of doom. I couldn't sleep without some kind of help, but knew that I would not pass the piss test in the morning. I hadn't had any sleep in about thirty hours and still I was too wired to keep my eyes closed for even a minute. I knew I was not going to relax until I was on a plane and off the ground!

I remember lying on a cot my last night in Vietnam believing the Viet Cong were planning a rocket attack, and there was a great big "X" painted on the roof over my head.

I spent the night with my eyes wide open and jumping up at every sound. When the sun rose, I was up and dressed, eager to piss for God and Country. A couple hours later I was on a roll call list for a flight roster on Flying Tiger Air Lines. I had my duffel bag, no drugs, no war souvenirs, just my Buddha carved from Marble Mountain in Da Nang (hand-painted by Don that seemed so long ago) and dirty clothes. I was eager to take my second piss test hopeful that I would pass that one. I remember looking out at that airplane like it was just yesterday.

Leaving the country was a last insult for all of us. There was no officer or politician to shake our hands. There were two MPs doing body searches at the foot of the stairs into the airplane. It was just like a big drug bust with everyone up against the wall! Halfway through my body search one of the MP's pulled an AK-47 round from my neck, I had been wearing it so long I forgot I even had it on. I argued with the MP over the property and the MP was very understanding. "Shut the fuck up or the plane will be leaving with one empty seat," were his final words. They worked. I surrendered that roach clip made from an AK-47 round. I found my seat and stared out into the night for my last look at Vietnam, not sure if peace outweighed the rage in my soul.

Either way, I thought, at least the war is over for me.

There was no cheering as the plane took off down the runway; there was just an eerie, if not downright spooky silence. The whole flight to Seattle was remarkably quiet. I suppose we all were reliving the past year. What had we done right to be on a plane heading home in one piece? Seattle was no different than Cam Rahn Bay. There were no bands and no politicians looking to pose for pictures with a returning Vietnam veteran. We were rushed off the plane into the night, taken into a mess hall, and awarded a steak dinner. After dinner we were officially welcomed home and given a lecture on the political climate of America the Beautiful. We were advised to wear civilian clothes in travel. If we choose to travel in uniform, we should be on our best behavior in spite of any comments we may receive from the civilian population that did not understand our mission in the Republic of South Vietnam.

Before we had any time to think about this little tidbit of information we had a lecture from the re-up NCO. He reminded us that we all had an excellent future as career soldiers and now was a great time to discuss our careers in the U.S. Army. As soon as the laughter died down he asked for a show of hands of those planning to re-enlist. I guess it was a matter of timing, none of us could think beyond the next twenty-four hours.

As the re-up NCO left mumbling to himself, we were taken to a large warehouse to be fitted for new Class A uniforms. By this time anything looked better than the jungle fatigues we were wearing. Once fitted in our neat new suits, our next stop was the travel department to make arrangements for our various flights across America.

Some of us dressed in our brand new dress greens, wearing Vietnam campaign ribbons proudly, and with airplane tickets in our hands, we were finally ready to go home. One-by-one our names were called and a clerk came out with our leave papers. One-by-one we arranged for transportation to the airport. We were on our way home.

It started the moment I walked into the main terminal of the Seattle Airport.

I could sense everyone staring at me. No one made any attempt to talk to me; in fact it was more like they were afraid that I might talk to them. I went straight to my flight, boarded my plane, and again found myself staring out the window into space. From Seattle to San Antonio no one said a word to me. We had a layover in San Antonio and once again I was wandering through an airport. I still was wearing my dress greens proudly, and somewhat naively expecting a pat on the back. I went into one of the lounge bars and ordered a beer. I couldn't believe it when the bartender asked for an ID.

I said, "My uniform is my ID. I just came back from Vietnam and I believe I am at least entitled to buy a beer without a hassle."

I did not impress him, as he put it, "I don't give a fuck where you spent your last year. You're in the state of Texas now and if you cannot show me a driver's license that shows you are twenty-one, get the fuck out of here."

I just stormed out. I was getting a sick feeling in my stomach and felt like throwing up.

I still had this odd feeling that everyone in the airport was staring at me as I made my way to a restroom. After losing half of my stomach, I threw some water over my face. Looking in the mirror I instantly decided to change. I had a Jesus Christ Superstar t-shirt and an old pair of jeans in my carry-on bag. I quickly changed, messed up my hair with water, tossed my uniform, and went back into the terminal.

I still had about an hour to kill so I went into a lounge and ordered a beer. This time I got a friendly, "How are you doing?" The guy sitting next to me even asked where I was from. It was like I was a whole different person than I was a few minutes before. I completed my flight to Boston in my civilian clothes. It felt like the mental apprehension against me had been left the plane. Before I even realized it we were over Boston Harbor.

Looking down at Boston Harbor, it was hard to believe that I was home. I was in the terminal waiting for my luggage when it dawned on me that I did not know my family's new street number or apartment number. I did not even know their new telephone number. I tried to get my mother's new number from an operator, but was told that it is an unlisted number. I explained that I just came back from Vietnam and was at the airport trying to reach my family.

Once again I got the message that being in Vietnam meant less than nothing. The operator said, "It doesn't matter where you are or where you were, I cannot release an unlisted number, goodbye."

I went back to get my luggage. At least I had my new address in my bag. No bag.

At the baggage claim I was told not to worry about it as they would track it down. Just call the lost and found department in the morning. I went out and got a cab to Memorial Drive Mystic Avenue Housing Project, Somerville. The cab driver asked me what number. All I could say was, "Your guess is as good as mine." He asked where I was coming from. I replied softly, "The Republic of South Vietnam." He didn't say another word after that but he did take the longest possible route from Logan Airport to Mystic Ave in Somerville. I got out of the cab at the beginning of the street, and asked a couple of kids, who looked like they were my brothers' age, if they knew where I lived. Of course, they even knew the apartment number. I was home — sort of. It was like a sixth sense telling me that I would never be home and it was right.

Scorpions, Monkeys and a Wild Night on a Fire Base

Small things sometimes bring back old memories of the war. The other day my son asked me, "Why are you so afraid of my pet scorpion?" As my mind wandered off into the past I told him I did not fear his pet, I just didn't like scorpions. I recalled a day back in 1971; I was pulling into Fire Base Vandergrift late from my mail run. It was dusk as I started to unload the mail and official correspondence. I was about half unloaded when I heard the new lieutenant screaming my name as he was rushing in my direction. He had only been in country a couple of weeks and was quite confused. He informed me without hesitation that I was to report for Listening Post Detail ASAP!

Listening Post Detail consisted of spending the night on the wrong side of the perimeter keeping a vigil for any enemy movement. Without hesitation, I told the young lieutenant to go and fuck himself. I explained that I was going to sort the battalion's mail and correspondence, and deliver them to the company clerks. Or, I told the wide-eyed lieutenant, I could inform all the company clerks that he had canceled all mail deliveries for the day. I also told him that if I spend the night bug-eyed in the middle of the jungle they would be no mail run tomorrow. Showing some signs of intelligence, he clutched his duty roster list to his chest, turned around, and wandered off.

It was a few hours later, after I had finally completed getting all the mail to the companies, that I found out who was sent out on Listening Post in my place. Maybe it was a feeling of guilt, but for some reason I spent the rest of the night in a bunker on the edge of the perimeter.

It was the first time I ever looked through a starlight scope into the heavily tree-covered mountains that surrounded our base. It was through the starlight scope that we first noticed what looked like a campfire far off in the jungle. We were in the middle of calling for some artillery, when we heard a scream from one of the men on Listening Post.

"I'm hit, I'm hit," was all we heard. We were not even sure which post was on the radio. The big tent on the edge of the perimeter had nothing in it but showers and used fatigues. Almost spontaneously, one side of the perimeter defense poured fire into and around the shower tent as artillery poured into the side of the mountain. At this point we heard screaming directly in front of us, "We are coming in. Get a medic now. We're coming across the perimeter now, get a medic!"

Within seconds we could see a dark figure dragging another figure over his shoulder. As soon as they got across the perimeter the whole side of the fire base opened up in a massive show of firepower. With all the noise and confusion going on it was hard to finally to understand the screaming. The soldier that had dragged his partner in was screaming at the medic, "You fuck'n idiot. I said, he was bit, not hit!"

As we looked on the medic yelled out, "Fuck'n scorpion!" He gave the man a shot and started treatment for shock. As he was being placed on a Dust-off chopper the firing around the fire base was dying down.

Sunrise finally brought some peace and quiet to the fire base. Dave had come within a minute of suffocating to death due to the effects of the scorpion's bite. A report from a recon over the mountain area we hit stated we had hit a group of deserters from an ARVN unit in Laos. The sorry bastards had little choice — die from North Vietnam artillery or American artillery! The shower tent area was full of dead bodies, too. The official body count was sixteen; the bodies of playful monkeys that made the mistake of meeting modern men, and his wonderful new inventions. Oh, and of course, there was one dead scorpion.

As I packed Dave's personal belongings and filled out his change of address card to the hospital down south, I wondered if I would have been better off if I had just gone out on the Listening Post.

Counting the Dead

The dead are in the earth, part of the earth, in the skies, in the eyes and soul of the living. Most of my life I have quietly stood on the sidelines counting the dead and wounded. My earliest memories of death are a mixture of dreams and the world of the living. I was out of sight and sound of my parents, away at summer camp, when my grandfather died. My oldest brother was also gone when I returned home. It was my first taste of death and abandonment.

Grandpa had no control of his leaving me nor did my brother; it simply was time to go. Grandpa had worn out his old body. My brother had tired of the abuse from my father and joined the service. My second oldest brother was alive and well, a ghost-like figure coming into my bed at night. Other nights I would sleep at my grandmother's house. In the middle of the night I would see a familiar robed figure — my grandfather at the foot of my bed trying to talk to me. From Charlestown we moved to Columbia Point housing project where death became commonplace. I recall gang fights and the bay littered with dead bodies, still strapped in their seats after a plane crash. I can still remember the fireman hosing down blood from the street after one of the trucks that continually raced in and out of the dump at the end of the projects had killed a girl chasing a ball.

By the age of thirteen we were living in Charlestown again. My favorite new book was *Profiles In Courage*. My favorite new song was *PT 109*. For the first time in my life I had a hero. I only met John Kennedy once while he was campaigning in Boston. He bought a newspaper from me and told me to stay in school. It was not long after meeting my hero, who had fought in the same war as my father, that I was selling newspapers with the headline, "President Kennedy Shot Dead."

By the age of fifteen we had moved again. We were living in Somerville. I was pondering the insanity of Charles Manson and his followers, and wondering why the only person I had a death wish for was still alive. My so-called brother was still controlling much of my life causing much sexual and moral confusion in my life. By the end of 1969, I had seen Robert Kennedy and Martin L. King killed for the crime of caring too much. Our class present to the high school was a tombstone dedicated to our dead in Vietnam. In December of 1969, I joined the Army and in July, 1970, I landed in Vietnam. The dead zone — I could start counting the dead in earnest!

At the time I am writing this it's 1995. It's my mother-in-law's seventy-sixth birthday. She lies next to me as I write this, sleeping in a bed in my living room next to my desk where I express my feeling through a word-processor. She has lost most of her bodily functions, as well as much of her will to live. How I can help her, I wonder as I sit in front of my keyboard. I don't recall what day it actually was, but I do remember a day in 1971 when I tried to count all the dead. I believe it was on February 25th — the day I counted the dead.

I started the day with the news that Highway Nine, the only way to get to Highway One, was still being swept for mines. I smoked one of those half-and-half menthol cigarettes: half tobacco, half a white powder common to the area. I soothed my throat with a shot of sour mash as I gazed up at the sky. Caravans of CH-54 equipment-moving helicopters were directly overhead, their cargo nets full of the dead from the fighting in Laos.

As I sipped my breakfast I wondered, how many bodies can each net hold?

I didn't have much time to ponder my question. The road was wide open and my services were needed. Part of my outgoing mail was ten packages — all which remained of ten dead members of our noble effort to shut down the trail of supplies pouring from Laos into South Vietnam.

The house is quiet. My mother-in-law is in a dead sleep as I become lost in my thoughts. Some nights, death just follows me around, blaming me for still living, seeking answers, and asking me why.

We left the fire base and headed down the dirt road around the mountains through the "Rockpile." Death was everywhere: a dead ARVN by the side of road; a pile of dead VC stacked up for public view down the road.

Death — you can smell it, see it, and sense it coming. It's just there. I lost my death count by mid-morning. I picked up my incoming mail and headed back in a daze with my packages of life from the real world. In a haze of smoke we cut off Highway One to Highway Nine only to see a sky full of heavy black smoke off in the distance. The road was full of the half-dead and half-living on a slow march south. A village that was alive and full in the morning was now dead and burning. I went back to my death count once again pondering how many people died. I didn't care why anymore, just how many dead were there. As we pulled into the fire base, once again I looked up into the sky to see more cargo nets full of the dead from the fighting in Laos.

As I was reflecting on how many bodies the nets were holding, when the scream "incoming" brought me back to the time and space I was in.

"Incoming…incoming!"

The scream preceded the sound of a rockets impact as I dove into a bunker. I was more involved with saving my own life, than reflecting on the dead. I stopped counting the dead and just sat in the bunker clutching my M-16, wondering if I was going to be one of the dead and possibly help increase the count.

As I sat waiting for my turn to die, the rockets stopped and I was blessed with another day to count the dead. Needless-to-say, I never did make it to the weekly casualty report.

No, today I am back in the world sitting in a dark room watching a sickly old woman, who is so afraid of death, and trying to understand her fear of something I know so well.

July 15, 1971 my last day in Vietnam (part two of the poem)

I was fearless, nothing could kill me,

I was so old that last day in Vietnam

I was driven south to Cam Ranh Air Base from Quang Tri Providence

where I had spent the last year

I felt naked without my M16, my bandolier and hand grenades

I was fearless; I was so old, that last day

heading south on Highway one.

No sniper could touch me; no land mine could touch me I arrived in Cam Ranh Bay totally stoned

I presented my end of tour orders my ticket back to the world

step one donate a cup of pee

no one leaves Vietnam with drugs in their system I realized that I should not have smoked

that Newport packed with heroin my last night in Vietnam

I was fearless, I was so old, and nothing mattered

drinking coffee, throwing up for a day or two

then another pee test I was on my way

I was on the tarmac in filthy Jungle Fatigues Boots packed
with mud Tiger Airlines my Freedom Bird

two M.P's do a body search No one leaves Vietnam with drugs
one of the MP's asks: "What is on the chain around your
neck?" he pulls out my AK 47 round, he calls it "contraband"

and says that I cannot leave with it

I tell him that I have a personal connection to it "It came out
of a jammed AK 47 that saved my life The dead gook* did
not need it anymore."

He says; "Nice story, but you have a choice of handing it over

or we can watch you freedom bird leave without you, as we
discuss the matter."

I was so fearless, I was so old. I just wanted to go home I said:
"It means nothing" I handed it over.

The plane lifts off, in an eerie silence

we are fearless, nothing could kill us we are so old, now

I spent the last 48 hours looking for Jesse

I did not find him

I cannot get him out of my head

I do not even know what his real name is We land in Alaska
for a lay over

most of us are old but still not old enough no alcohol allowed
by the airport

back on board heading for Seattle /Tacoma there's is more
chatter now as we share

our dreams of home and peace

for a moment we are young once again In the safety of the

nights darkness

we are hoarded off the plane into buses

taken to Fort Lewis

a steak dinner the fastest tailors on the face of Earth working 24 hours a day

In the morning we will all have perfect fitting Dress Greens complete with Battle Ribbons and a Combat Patch

a hot shower, and a real bed though sleep is impossible to quiet

in the morning we are sharp in our new Dress Greens

a chest full of Battle Ribbons we are fearless, we are so old

our tickets for our flights home in hand one last word of advice

From an old Top Sargent:

"We advise you to travel in civvies wearing your uniform, might cause

a disturbance at the airport."

I am fearless, I am old

I am going to fly back to Boston wearing my Dress Greens

I am Billy the Kid.

The Pilgrim — Chapter Thirty Three

In his song, *Pilgrim, Chapter 33*, Kris Kristofferson says he wrote the song about various celebrities; two of those mentioned, Johnny Cash and Dennis Hopper. He later performed the song on *The Johnny Cash Show* saying "Epitaph" is about Janis Joplin. Throughout the early seventies, *Pilgrim; Chapter 33* was playing over and over on my turntable, and in my head the lines:

"He's a walkin' contradiction,

partly truth and partly fiction.

Taking every wrong direction on his lonely way back home

See him wasted on the sidewalk in his jacket and his jeans:

Wearing' yesterday's misfortunes like a smile … "

That just was me in the middle 1970s, in my army field jacket and jeans…wearing my Vietnam memories like a smile, stoned most of the time, my wartime stories partly true…partly fiction, a walking contradiction.

Bob Hope, Jane Fonda: Heroes or Villains?

The faces are aging, but still every time I see Jane Fonda's phony actress smile or Bob Hope's standard grin I cringe. The sound of their voices or the mere uttering of their names sends me back in time. Hanoi Jane was easy to hate without any explanation. How many American military personnel died because Jane's visit to Hanoi convinced the leaders of North Vietnam that America had no willpower or the determination to fight very long to save the Republic of South Vietnam. Jane and her followers eventually convinced Nixon and Kissinger to give the Communist regime anything they wanted at the Paris peace talks.

The other familiar face, Mr. Hope, is a lot more complicated. How can anyone hate Bob Hope? So many people ask me after all he has done for America's troops. The question I have asked myself over the years is — did Mr. Hope do the USO tours to keep his career alive, or out of the kindness of his heart?

I recall the day Bob Hope came to Camp Eagle in 1970. I was relaxing in front of my hooch, enjoying a little smoke, listening to Country Joe and the Fish, and reading *Love Story*. I was just quietly day-dreaming about being back in

Cambridge. My moment of peace came to a sudden end when I heard the executive officer screaming at people that they had a top priority assignment for the next day. It turned out that the high command was upset that Bob Hope could be embarrassed by a lack of interest in his current USO tour. To relate to this you have to think about the situation.

It was 1970, Bob Hope was a leftover from the song and dance acts of the 1930's when the U.S. government saved his career after being used as a morale booster during World War II. See Bob tell a few old jokes, see him kiss the hottest new actresses direct from the big screen, see a parade of semi-nude dancers, and then go back to the war in a better mood.

After the "Good War," Mr. Hope made a string of second-rate movies, and once again his shining star was in decline. Along came the Korean War and Bob Hope was back as the U.S. government's main USO show. A special gift for all the troops in Korea. Bob was a star again with a huge network contract and more movies. Throughout my early years, the late 50s and early 60s, Bob Hope's smiling face in a wave of men and women in uniform was a common sight on network television.

By the middle-60s the television specials were full of the same old jokes and skits, and the ratings were going down. Bob was making possibly the worst movies of his career. Vietnam came along and once again the U.S. government supplied an all-expense paid trip to a war to film more smiling, waving men and women in uniform. The network gave him another big contract and more Christmas specials from the war. By the 1970's there wasn't a white soldier in Vietnam who had not seen one of Mr. Hope's specials while in high school. We heard our fathers laugh at the old jokes and giggle as the dirty old man of comedy kissed some young new actress. Boston's old Howard was gone, but Bob Hope was bringing the old tits-and-ass, song-and-dance shows to network television. In fact, in 1970 Mr. Hope owned a good portion of the most valuable land in California and was one of the richest men in the country.

So there I was, as comfortable as you can get in Vietnam, when click, the executive officer shut Country Joe off right in the middle of my favorite song, *Fixing to Die Rag*. First, he asked me how I could listen to that crap, then he got on my nerves. As he was writing my name on his clipboard he informed me that I was going to be a volunteer to see the Bob hope show in the morning. There would be a formation at 0900 and I was to be there.

The thought sent a chill down my spine — all those semi-naked women dancing around. Then the thought of Bob Hope and those same old jokes hit me. I declined the offer much to the dismay of the executive officer. He screamed, "What? You do not want to see the Gold Diggers? What are you a fag or something?"

I refused to discuss my sex life. I just reminded him that the next day was Sunday and I never missed Mass. He informed me that the chaplain and his assistant were going to be at the show. I informed him that I was going to the chapel to pray unless he gave me a direct order to go to the Bob Hope show. I told him I seen the act already, and it was old and boring.

He looked me in the eyes for a very long time then put a line through my name. He called me a fag again, muttered something about my Communist music, and then went on his way. Bob packed them in a huge smiling crowd, waving and shouting, "We love you, Bob." There were "There's hope with Hope" signs. A perfect Bob Hope special brought more profits for Mr. Hope so he could buy up more of California.

What can you do? It was the only show in town. The U.S. government was not going to fly Country Joe and the Fish or The Doors over to put on a show for the troops.

The day of the show was the quietest and most pleasant day I spent in the Republic of South Vietnam. The area was like a ghost town from the Old West — rows and rows of empty hoochs. The Dust-off choppers sat silently on the helicopter pads. The smell of cooking flowed out of my hooch. The aroma of good smoke filled the air, the taste of bourbon, and quiet conversation with a good friend, along with two beautiful hooch maids.

Thanks, Bob, for giving me this blissful day. Tomorrow I will go back to the war.

Bob Hope at Camp Eagle, Christmas week, December, 1970

A special thank you

to Chris Makary, the staff and fellow vets from the
Boston VAOPC's Veterans Improvement Program

In healing a wounded Heart, and Mind.

CPSIA information can be obtained at www.ICGtesting.com
Printed in the USA
LVOW05s1814010414

379536LV00009B/2/P